Training Management
A Practical Guide

Also by Steven A. Schwarzman

Technical Writing Management: A Practical Guide

Training Management
A Practical Guide

Steven A. Schwarzman

Training Management: A Practical Guide

Copyright © 2012 by Steven A. Schwarzman

All rights reserved. No part of this book may be reproduced, distributed, or transmitted in any form or by any means, electronic or mechanical, including photocopying, recording, or by any information storage and retrieval system, without permission in writing from the publisher, except for brief quotations in a book review.

Portions of this book previously appeared in *Technical Writing Management: A Practical Guide* by the same author.

ISBN-13 978-1479302277

ISBN-10 1479302279

First Edition

Contents

Chapter 1   Introduction   1

    A guide for training managers   1

    Becoming a training manager   2

    Training as a business   2

    Trainers who become managers   2

    Managers who are not trainers   3

    Freelance training consultants   4

    Training agency owners   4

    What's in this book   5

Chapter 2   Training for new managers   7

    A quick intro to training   7

    Training is task-based   8

    Managing training in your organization   9

    Managing training development   10

    Training and product management   10

    Training and debugging   12

       Managing the bug reporting process   12

Formal bug reporting	13
Informal bug reporting	13
What skills do trainers need?	15
Familiarity with subject areas	15
Writing skills	18
Analytical skills	18
Information skills	19
People and presentation skills	20
Starting a combined training and documentation group	21
Getting started as a training manager	21
How to do training	21
Training program components	22
Chapter 3 How to do a training needs analysis	23
Identify the groups of learners	25
Identify each group's training needs	26
Build a list of lessons needed	28
Associate the lessons to the groups	30
Analyze delivery needs	31
Geography	31
Numbers of learners	32

Languages	34
Schedules	35
Create a budget	37
Direct costs	37
Indirect costs	37
Adjust the budget to needs and constraints	38
Other budget considerations	39
Approve or obtain approvals	40

Chapter 4 Training development — 43

Build on a straight line	43
Make the training task-based	43
Train common tasks, not exceptions	45
Include necessary prerequisites	47
Structuring your training lessons	48
Introduction	48
Lesson Objective	48
Why You Need to Know	49
Tasks	50
Exercises	50
Review or Quiz	51
Instructor Guides	53

Presentations	53

Chapter 5 Training delivery — 55

Choose a delivery method: instructor-led or online	55
Classroom training: instructor-led	57
Online learning	59
Set the tone: fun exploration	60
Training delivery management	60

Chapter 6 Training evaluation — 63

The Kirkpatrick model	63
Level one – reaction	63
Level two – learning	64
Level three – behavior	65
Level four – results	66
How to create evaluation questionnaires	67
Communicate the evaluations	69

Chapter 7 How to hire trainers — 73

Establish the requirements	73
Interview stakeholders	74
Consult with human resources	75
Define the business goal: why are you hiring?	76

Put the criteria together	77
Evaluate the resumes	93
Interview the trainers	95
Questions to ask about a candidate's education	95
Questions to ask about a candidate's resume	96
Review the samples	98
Give a test	101
The purpose of a test	102
Designing a good test	103
When to test	105
A sample test	106

Chapter 8   Managing a training group in a corporate environment   109

The role of trainers in a corporate environment	109
Educate your trainers	110
Educate your company	110
How to be professional when others aren't	112
The training team	113
Define standards	115
Distribute the work in your team	123
The manager as editor	124

Peer editing	124
Dedicated editors	125
Involve the trainers	125
Build teams	127
Monitor the work and communications	129
Evaluate the trainers	132
Formal evaluations can be a wasteful process	132
Align evaluations with your hiring criteria	133
Transparent evaluations	134
Client relations	135
Business to consumer	135
Business to business	139
Serving customers directly	140
Offering customized training	142
Serving as a bridge to the customer	143
Helping customers with their own internal training	143
Communicating with other groups in your organization	144
Re-use, repurposing, and content management systems	145

Chapter 9 Estimating, tracking, and managing training projects 149

Determine the project scope 149

Estimates and schedules 150

Define the deliverable and its scope 151

Create an outline 152

Analyze the topics 152

Define a multiplier for your work: how many hours does it take you to write a page? 155

Do the math: create a rough estimate for your project 157

Refine the estimate: build and iteratively refine an estimating formula that works 158

Analyze completed projects to refine the formula still more 160

Why it's important to use a formula 161

Sample variables to use in your formula 162

How the formula helps you in internal and external sales 166

Estimates as input to project plans 167

Estimates as input to pricing 167

Assemble the project team 168

Deploying existing internal staff 169

Deploying existing staff trainers from another group in your organization	170
Augmenting your staff with contract trainers	172
Augmenting your staff with permanent new hires	173
Writing a staffing plan	175
Provide resources and leadership	177
Working with outsourced trainers or outsourced SMEs	181
Track and report	183
Reporting to management	183
Reporting to peers	184
Reporting to your team	184
Project management software	184
Training program communication	186
Deliver the project	186
Evaluate the project	188
Evaluate project stats	188
Analyze variances from your estimates	188
Evaluate the human side of the project	189
Communicate project results	190

A Practical Guide   xiii

Chapter 10   Running a training business   191

   Finding jobs   191

      Targeting companies to be your clients   192

      When HR is your client   195

      Solo contractors: writing your training resume   197

      Training resume bloopers   200

      Training job sites   204

      Jobs with training agencies   207

      Agencies and the IRS: whose employee are you?   208

      The agency business model   209

      Alternative agencies   210

      Choosing an agency   211

   Marketing yourself as a freelance trainer   213

      Creating and maintaining a training web site   215

      E-mail as a marketing tool   220

      Business cards   221

      Active marketing techniques   221

   Other marketing avenues   224

   Managing your clients   225

      The paper trail lifecycle of client management   226

      Maintaining personal contact   235

Chapter 1
Introduction

A guide for training managers

There are many books available on the techniques of training, primarily for beginners and practitioners of training. But there are very few books on how to manage the training group in a company or how to manage a training business (whether you're on your own as a freelancer or you have trainers working for you). If you are a trainer who manages other trainers, or especially if you are a non-trainer who manages trainers, this book is for you.

It's not my intention to duplicate information you can easily get in other places. So, for example, the sections on managing training projects show a methodology specific to training. If you want to learn general management and project management techniques, and you should, there are resources available elsewhere that don't need to be replicated here. What this book aims for is to provide you as a manager of training with the specifics that you need to succeed and that you won't easily find elsewhere.

Secondarily, this book aims to give new managers, and future managers, a leg up on how to actually run a training group, based on some 20 years of experience in the field.

Becoming a training manager

There are different situations in which someone becomes a manager of a training group. Sometimes a trainer grows into the role within a company as the department grows, sometimes trainers are subsumed under some other group – I've seen trainers belonging to support, HR, sales, testing, marketing, documentation, consulting, and infrastructure groups – and the person in charge of training in the company isn't actually a trainer and may never have been one.

Training as a business

Trainers who set up their own freelance business have their own specific needs: not only are they the managers, they're also the trainers. Finally, owners or managers of training agencies, whether or not they happen to be trainers themselves, have management issues specific to a training business to consider.

Trainers who become managers

If you are a trainer, one day you may find yourself being asked to manage a training group. How do you go about learning the mysterious new tasks of managing people, projects, and budgets when all you've had to do up to now has been managing a class?

You can read general books on management, but trainers are a special breed, and the nature of assignments, workloads, and expectations in a training group tend to be particular.

How do you assert your new authority? The simple answer is that you don't. "New manager syndrome" occurs when a new boss feels it necessary to show everyone who's boss, and the only way they can think of to do that is by barking orders left and right. Far better to establish yourself as a manager and leader by getting down to business in managing the work your group needs to produce, helping your trainers overcome the obstacles lying in ambush along the critical path of the project, and showing that you are leading the team toward a vision that you can and do articulate. Respect can only be earned.

Managers who are not trainers

If you are a manager of a training group, but not a trainer yourself, how do you figure out how to hire good trainers? How do you manage a training project? What's different about working with trainers, and what issues do they commonly face?

You may know management, but this training group that your VP gave you to run seems to speak its own language, and at least some of the trainers have very different perspectives on the company than the programmers or engineers or testers or sales people or consultants that you're used to managing.

Freelance training consultants

If you're a freelance or contract trainer, how do you run your business, from marketing to estimating projects to billing? You're a one-person shop, and your ability to manage the business end of things will determine your success. You have to be able to estimate and manage projects precisely, and you have to keep track of your time so that you can bill your clients and get paid. Even before all this, you have to find those clients, and that may not come to you easily.

Training agency owners

Most training agency owners are former trainers and have worked as freelancers (or as contractors with another agency) before they open up their own agencies.

Even so, the day-to-day needs of running the business and trying to build it up through difficult economic cycles may make another perspective welcome.

What's in this book

The chapters that follow aim to address these issues:

Chapter 2 is a quick overview of training, including both training development and training delivery for non-trainer managers.

Chapter 3 walks you through the process of conducting a training needs analysis to identify who and what needs to be trained.

Chapter 4 guides you in managing the training development process so you can build training courses that meet the needs you identify in your training needs analysis.

Chapter 5 covers training delivery methods from a management perspective, so you can select the methods that work best for each project you do.

Chapter 6 is about training evaluation – how to get the most useful information you can to evaluate and improve your training.

Chapter 7 is a guide on how to hire trainers to fit your particular organization's needs, from establishing your real requirements to evaluating resumes and samples, interviewing, and testing.

Chapter 8 covers a variety of issues in ongoing management of a training group, including standards, work distribution models, communicating, and evaluation processes. It also includes a section on client relations.

Chapter 9 is about estimating, tracking, and managing projects in your training group, with a detailed methodology to help you build your own accurate estimates and bring your projects in on time and budget. It also offers guidance on how to staff up for projects.

Chapter 10 is about running a training *business*: finding clients, working with agencies, job sites, resumes, marketing, and the lifecycle of marketing, sales, and project management documents.

Chapter 2
Training for new managers

A quick intro to training

Training isn't education.

Education has the lofty goal of transferring knowledge and its methods of acquisition to those who have not yet learned a particular subject. It's what you learn in college, or at least what you *could* have been learning.

Training, on the other hand, has a far more limited purpose: transferring non-theoretical knowledge on how to do something. When you train someone, you want them to be able to do something that they couldn't do before, or do it better, or make fewer errors.

Training might be on how to use a new software system. Or it might be on how to fill out the new timesheet. Or how to overcome objections in the sales process. Or how to greet customers on the phone. Or how to administer the company travel policy. Or how to fly the plane when an engine gives out. Or how to sell more of the company's products or services using a time management program. Or how to raise funds for your nonprofit organization.

Unlike education, training always has specific goals in mind. Training does not try to create renaissance men and women. It aims to solve specific, defined problems. Training can be measured in terms of its outcomes, and indeed these outcomes define any training plan from the start.

Training is task-based

The best training is task-based. When you create a training program, you need to focus on what your learners need to *learn*. And that's not the same thing as "everything there is to *know* about" whatever subject you're training.

For example, say you're creating a training program for a new software system. The system has five or six menus, and dozens of screens, buttons, and other good stuff. Your job as a training manager is to discern what *tasks* different groups of people will need to know how to perform in the system – and that's not about the system at all.

It's about designing a training course – or several courses for different kinds of users – so that the sales people learn how to do what they need to do *using* the system, and the same with the sales support people, and the clerical people, and the A/R people, and so on

– with each group using different parts of the system to achieve different goals. Training isn't about the menus and screens. It's about the tasks relevant for each kind of user and how they are to accomplish those tasks with the system.

In a word, training has to be relevant.

Managing training in your organization

As a manager, you need to know the purpose of training *in your organization*. Usually, it's not about teaching every aspect of whatever the subject is. It's usually about helping learners, or trainees, know or find out how to know what they need to know in order to get their jobs done. Sometimes, there's some theory involved. But most of the time, training is practical learning.

You also need to understand your training developers and trainers and how they interact with the rest of the company. Training, much like documentation, is often something of an afterthought in overall project planning – that is, the planning of the larger projects in which training is one of many components – but one of your responsibilities as a manager is to change this, to the extent possible in your context, for the benefit of the organization.

And it's not so much about changing opinions directly in a public relations campaign; more effective is to establish good working relations with other groups, supporting them and getting their support for your team.

Managing training development

Unless your training team is charged with training only external tools or skills – think third-party software or skills classes that you purchase ready-to-use – your group will need to engage in the art of training development, meaning that they will be creating training programs and not just delivering them.

Your trainers and the people they work with in your organization to create training programs are partners, working at different stations on the assembly line. Content decisions are not always the trainer's responsibility, so your trainers may have to defer sometimes to Sales, or IT, or whoever owns that domain content. But your trainers are there to help the domain owners, and if you go about it the right way, the domain owners will more than appreciate all the improvements and fixes your group brings about before the training materials go out.

Training and product management

As a manager, you need to know why your company or organization has a training group. In some cases, training groups actually produce direct revenue in the form of sales of training programs and services. In some companies, though, training is seen as a cost center, not a profit center. This is the case where training is thrown in as a free incentive to buy the overall system or product.

So why do companies bother with a training department (and its cousin, a documentation department)?

The answer is that training is part of the product. And companies that offer a better product will, over time, begin to win business away from those offering an inferior product, other factors being equal.

Bad or missing training and documentation can have a direct and negative effect on sales. Conversely, good training and documentation make for smoother implementations of complex products. Smooth implementations make for happy customers and help support sales. Trainers are also sometimes used to demonstrate products in a presales phase.

Training and documentation serve another bottom-line purpose, though this one is harder to measure. Good training and documentation, along with good product design, reduce support costs. The more users are able to figure out the product based on intuitive design, training on the basics, and available help, the less they have to contact your support department.

So training makes financial sense. And since users correctly perceive them as part and parcel of the product itself, training and documentation should be integrated into the product. Product management really includes the training and the documentation, too.

Training and debugging

One of the most conspicuous side-benefits of a good training team is that as they work with the product and its design documentation, they will discover bugs and design flaws in the product before it is released. In some companies, the training group (especially if it is organizationally part of the documentation group) can open bug reports in the same bug tracking system that the developers use. In others, the process is less formal.

Managing the bug reporting process

Either way, your role as the training manager is to make sure this process takes place the way it should. If your group is opening trouble tickets, the development teams will be very aware of this. They may even dispute what your trainers report. After all, they are usually under significant pressure to debug the problems they already know about in a short time frame, and your group will be adding to the list.

Here is where you come in. As a manager, you need to establish through clear communication with your colleagues in development that your trainers are knowledgeable enough to accurately know a bug when they see one, and not just flood the tracking system with "bugs" that turn out to be user error.

And, of course, this means that you have to make this assertion true.

Formal bug reporting

In order to do that, you may want to have your trainers come to you first before they report the suspected bug. Let them explain the problem to you, or show it to you as it occurs, or show the discrepancy between what the system does and what the spec says it is supposed to do, before you let them make the report.

Once you know that a trainer is able to do this on their own, you can step out of the way and let them work directly with development.

Informal bug reporting

Similar advice applies in informal bug-reporting scenarios, where the procedure is undefined and boils down to your trainers reporting to their developer colleagues. If they already have a good working relationship, then they can probably do fine by simply showing the problem directly to the SMEs (Subject Matter Experts, the people who own the domain content).

If they don't – and this can happen for a variety of reasons – then some thoughtful managerial action on your part may be in order. You might want to stroll over to the developer, if *you* have an existing relationship, or at least credibility as someone who knows the system or product, and casually bring the matter to the developer's attention. This may especially be appropriate if your trainer is new or new to the task at hand.

Other possible avenues are arranging meetings with the trainers and SMEs, preferably informal meetings where food is made available, or using phone calls, emails, and text messaging, as appropriate in your company. While emails are for good reason often not the medium of choice, because they can seem threatening even when they are not intended to be, there can be cases where they work better. Some developers hate interruptions. Some do not like talking to eager trainers. Technical people may prefer the batch queue-like inbox to allow them to work through reported issues on their own when convenient to them and using their own prioritization.

The better part of managing the communications between your trainers and the experts is knowing which methods work for which teams and which developers. Ultimately, by finding the bugs before the customers do, you and your team are helping the developers.

But remember that how you package this help will determine how well it is received. Be careful in reporting how many bugs you found, though it is both legitimate and helpful for you to let your management know what a big contribution your group makes. Just be sufficiently politic, and not unnecessarily confrontational, and the developers will come to value the contributions that your trainers make without feeling that their own abilities are being challenged by your group or that you have an agenda other than improving the product.

What skills do trainers need?

Trainers need to understand training. It's not rocket science, but if you don't understand how people learn, you will have a hard time building and delivering training programs for them.

And, in addition to training skills, trainers need to have knowledge in the domains that they train. Sales trainers need to understand the sales process. Technical trainers must be literate in the technologies they train. Soft-skills trainers need to understand and practice the soft skills they train. And so on.

Finally, trainers also need to be familiar with the tools of the training trade, both in terms of development tools – in some cases, that will mean nothing more than word processing and presentation software; in others, it will mean higher-end tools – and in terms of delivery tools.

Familiarity with subject areas

Trainers have to have a basic familiarity with the subjects they train and the industries they serve, by which I mean an educated layperson's sort of understanding, not necessarily mastery in all circumstances. But even more than a familiarity with subjects, curiosity and aptitude are critical components in a trainer's toolkit. If trainers can't fathom a new subject, even after reading background material, that's a pretty big problem.

For example, in the world of software training on a technical level – that is, training for programmers – this means that trainers must understand how software works, perhaps on a level one might pick up after a few semesters of a college programming course. I do mean *programming*, not the local community college's Computers Can Be Friendly Tools offering.

The specific language doesn't matter so much as long as trainers pick up an understanding of programming logic. Once they have this, they're set, because they can apply the same basic principles to the specific platforms they will be training.

I had a course in BASIC back in high school, and followed this up with a semester of FORTRAN in my freshman year of college. This was so long ago that we used keypunch machines to poke holes in cards. One card contained one line of code. A "program" was a stack of cards, held together by a rubber band. A complex program was a *big* stack of cards, held together by a fat rubber band. Running a program meant taking the stack of cards to the card reader, *very* carefully removing the rubber band, and putting the cards in the machine. The machine would mechanically go through the cards, noting the holes punched in each, send the program into the mainframe, and spit the cards out the other end. The process of collecting the cards and re-securing them with the rubber band was one of equal drama. Depending on the workload and whims of the mainframe operator, the results of the program in the form of a printout might be available 30 minutes or an hour later.

Archaic as this may seem now, this knowledge has been indispensable in my work as a trainer and documenter of software (not the keypunch part, but developing and debugging algorithms). Programs written on very different platforms years later still use the same basic principles of logic, because algorithms are algorithms. This means that when a systems analyst describes what a piece of software is supposed to do, I can follow the explanation intelligently, and I know what kinds of questions to ask to make sure I have understood. On some occasions, this process has resulted in improvements to the software, because I might bring up an angle that the developer had not considered.

The ability to read software code also is a big plus for a software trainer. It makes it possible for the trainer and the developer to speak the same language when the trainer can "look under the hood" of the car, so to speak, and understand what the mechanic has to say.

Writing skills

Trainers simply must have excellent writing skills, because their writing will go into the training deliverables.

A newspaper editor once spoke about a reporter who couldn't put an English sentence together properly, even though that was his first language. But he had excellent reporting abilities. He could find the right sources, and get the story, like nobody else could. As a result, the paper found it worthwhile to have someone edit the reporter's raw copy.

But trainers have no such luxury. While it is true that large projects can include a separate copy editing function, there is generally no time in the business world – especially the software world, where a product must usually be rushed out the door – to have an editor dedicated to fixing up bad writing. Editors in large projects are usually charged instead with the job of ensuring standardization in style and format.

Analytical skills

Perhaps the most important skill for a trainer is the ability to analyze and process information. What trainers really do, after all, is translate information from whatever the sources might be – engineers, programmers, other documents, or their own experimentation with the product – into a language, structure, and format that are accessible and appropriate for the intended audience.

In order to do that, they can't just spit out what they receive as inputs. (If you've seen help for a software application that doesn't offer anything beyond "Fill in the fields in this screen and click <OK>," you know what I'm talking about.) Trainers have to go far beyond that. They have to analyze what conditions brought the user to that screen in the first place – whether intentional navigation or not – and what they want to accomplish there. Then they have to analyze the information they've received about what happens there, with all the branching possibilities. Next, they must analyze – even map out – the best way to present the information they've gathered so as to be truly helpful to the user. Only then does writing of training materials begin.

Information skills

Trainers have to find the information. They can't sit back and wait for it to come to them – and believe me, I've seen trainers try to get by doing just that. They don't last long, because they don't add value.

To be able to find the information they need, sometimes trainers can rely on established procedures. If the module they're working on is number 37 in a series of similar training modules, they know that the methods that worked for numbers 1 through 36 will probably work here as well. But even that is not always the case. They have to hunt down and evaluate the information from all available sources – and perhaps some that *seem* unavailable – to get what they need.

Trainers are bloodhounds, and good ones have the ability to ferret out information even from badly-written specs and truncated, pressured interviews with subject matter experts, and especially through their own understanding of what the system must do even if the developer wasn't able to describe this well in any of the other information sources.

People and presentation skills

With the possible exception of asynchronous distance learning, trainers need to love people and love helping people learn. Trainers need to transfer a sense of excitement about learning to students who, in the context of learning a new system or work process, naturally have some degree of fear that needs to be overcome. And the calm, friendly presence of a trainer who is genuinely excited about learning and about how the new system will ultimately help the learners do their job better.

In classroom learning, trainers obviously need to love interacting with learners. It's not all about standing in front of a room and regaling people with funny anecdotes. But trainers do need to address the needs of their adult learners: training has to be interesting, sometimes even entertaining, and relevant. Armed with a well-developed training program, good trainers use that program to interact with their learners to achieve the goal: learning and knowledge transfer.

Starting a combined training and documentation group

In some companies, especially small ones, the training group may be asked to assist with documentation, or to create it if there is no documentation department. Who better than the trainers, who – if they're good – know the subject matter closely and have already created training modules intended for users of one sort or another?

Training and documentation don't have exactly the same goals. But, in the large scope of many organizations, they are closely enough related to each other for it to make sense to treat them as one entity, perhaps with different teams focusing on different products or on either the training or documentation side of things.

Getting started as a training manager

The chapters that follow are intended to guide you through the training process from your perspective as a training manager. You'll have to adjust the ingredients of this recipe based on your specific circumstances, but this book will give you a framework that you can plug those experiences and contingencies into.

How to do training

You can get a PhD in adult learning. Or, for the price of this book, I can teach you the basic idea in a sentence: adult learning is just like kid learning; it should be hands-on, interesting, and to the point. Kids love to learn how the world works, and so do adults, especially adults whose jobs require them to learn what you're training them to do. Now you can tell your friends that you have the equivalent of a PhD in adult learning!

Training program components

The two main components of a training program are development and delivery. Development refers to the creation of training materials, the stuff you're going to use in a physical or virtual class. Delivery refers to the method you're going to employ to deliver that content to the trainees.

It may be, in some cases, that you can buy your content off the shelf and skip developing it on your own, but we don't know that yet. Before you can decide this and other questions, you need to do a training needs analysis.

That's the first step in any training program, and can be done formally for a large rollout, or informally when the expense and trouble of a full-blown needs analysis can't be justified. How to do a training needs analysis is the subject of the next chapter.

Chapter 3
How to do a training needs analysis

The basic question that you ask in a training needs analysis is, who needs to learn what? Do you know what each of the relevant groups of people (your employees, your customers, or whoever the training audience is) needs to learn? Specifically, what can they *not* do now that they need to do in the future? That's the difference between training and education. You can go to school for an education – that is, new *knowledge*, but training means getting people to learn new *behaviors*.

Are you putting a new information security system in place? Are there new policies that people need to follow? Is there a problem with order handling, and you've been charged with reducing errors? The end result of your needs analysis is a spreadsheet of Who needs What – that is, which groups of people need to learn exactly which lessons. (Maybe one size fits all, maybe not.) If the population of trainees is spread out in multiple locations, note that, too, because it will be relevant in deciding on a delivery strategy. Also, if there are any special factors, like if some students require training in a different language, on a different schedule (night shift, different time zone, whatever), or anything else that will have an impact on the training itself, both development and delivery, note these as well.

Armed with your spreadsheet of who your learners are and what they need to learn, in full detail that you have analyzed, you are ready to do your development. At that point, you'll know if your needs can be met by a commercial training product. If so, skip to Training Delivery.

Without a training needs analysis, you would be left guessing: guessing how many learners there are, guessing what they need to learn, guessing about their geographical and time distributions, guessing about what the training program will cost, and, worst of all, guessing about whether the training program will have achieved its goals, because it is the training needs analysis that defines those goals.

To put it in terms of project management methodology, your training needs analysis results in your project plan. Until you have that, you don't have a complete picture of what you need to do and what decisions you will need to make in order to accomplish your goals optimally.

Identify the groups of learners

The first item in the training needs analysis is identifying the learners, the people who will be taking part in your training program.

In a system migration, that population is usually "everybody," meaning that all groups are affected by the change and will need training. But that's not good enough for the purpose here, because you need to break down that "everybody" into smaller groups that have individualized needs.

For example, the sales representatives will need training on using the front end of the new system as part of their sales preparation and presentation process. They will also need to learn how to view and interpret the new reports available.

Meanwhile, the sales support people back in the office will need training on everything the salespeople get, and at a more comprehensive level, because they will be providing first-level support to the sales reps. And the sales support staff will also need to learn the back-end parts of the system.

Sales managers need the same material as the sales reps, but they also need in-depth training on the reporting options plus training on the management functions such as assigning reps to accounts and overriding commission chargebacks for returns in warranted circumstances.

Outside of the sales organization, the finance department needs training on the new accounting, payroll, receivables, and general ledger applications in the new system, while the customer service group needs training on their part of the system.

For an enterprise-wide system, all these groups within the "everybody" who needs training have very distinct needs.

So the first step is simply to identify the groups, and then within each group, identify the numbers of learners of each subgroup. Using the sales reps as an example, you might find that there are 500 reps total, of whom 300 are based out of the central office, with another 100 in field and even home offices, and the remaining 100 not actual employees, but independent agents who are given access only to portions of the system. These different subgroups may well have differing needs for training.

Identify each group's training needs

Now that you have the groups themselves identified, the next step is to figure out what their training needs are. Unless you are an expert in all aspects of your organization's units and their work, you will need to interview relevant people in the organization to get this information. You can probably do some of this by email, but ultimately you will want to have conversations with the people to follow up and to make sure that you really do have an understanding of what each group does, and what it will do in the new system.

Using the example again of a system migration, what you need to zero in on is twofold: what the people will need to know how to do using the new system and, possibly, what their new workflows will be now that there is a new system. That is, sometimes new systems replace old ones and the workflows remain untouched. But more often, with a new system come new workflows and processes. It's easy to forget about these when developing a training program, but the workflows are arguably even more important than the system.

So, if the old workflow involved paper forms and faxes with manager signatures, and the new workflow instead automatically routes exceptions to managers for on-screen approvals, with routine cases approved automatically, all parties involved – the sales reps, the clerical support people, and the managers – need to know about this change, and so it has to be part of your training program. You can't assume that people will learn this by magic.

The business analysts and system analysts who designed the new system (or its implementation, if it isn't a custom system) are your friends. Talk to them to understand how each kind of user will be using the new system, and for what purposes. (You need to do this even if you know the *system*, because you need to find out how the various users will be using the system in the current implementation.) Read the documentation that they produce to describe workflows and system flows.

Verify what you read with the analysts and the implementation team to make sure that undocumented changes weren't made mid-process. In the vast majority of cases, such changes are indeed made as a project moves from theoretical to real; what doesn't always happen is that those changes get reflected in updated documents. So you do need to check.

Build a list of lessons needed

As you go through the documents – the design documents, the system flows, the user documents if they already exist – and as you meet with the analysts and representatives of each of the user types in your organization, record what it is that each needs to learn.

There will be some basic lessons that everyone, or at least multiple groups, will need to learn. And there will be some highly specific lessons that might apply only to very small groups of users, perhaps even fewer than ten people.

For all but the simplest training programs, this list of lessons will likely become large. So it is best to begin organizing it logically from the beginning, to reduce accidental overlaps and to reduce the likelihood of gaps going unidentified.

Continuing with the example from above, you might decide that the sales reps need the following lessons:

- Preparing Sales Calls
- Scheduling Customers
- Presenting Sales Proposals
- Overcoming Objections
- Using Alternative Proposals
- Reaching Agreement
- Capturing Approval
- Processing Forms
- Understanding Reports

These are all subjects that, being experienced reps, the sales people know how to do in the old system. But they need to learn the new ways to do these things in the new system. (Note that when you need to create updated training for new hires, not the experienced reps in this example, you'll need to expand the course to include your organization's methods and procedures.)

Of all the lessons in that list, probably the only one that will be shared with other groups is Understanding Reports, and even that one will likely focus on sales reports specifically. But if you organize your lessons well, you may be able to reuse material across multiple groups to achieve some savings. Certainly, for the subgroup within the sales organization that is sales managers, you can reuse all of the sales rep materials, with the addition of specific lessons that managers need.

For example, the additional lessons that managers might need could be:

- an extended Understanding Reports lesson (that includes the managerial reports that only they see)
- a lesson on how to reassign customers from one sales rep or team to another
- Approving Exceptions

If you can, keep all of the lesson names in one document, so that you can readily identify closely-related lessons across groups (and to make sure that you don't create two different lessons, one called Understanding Reports and another called Learning about Reports!).

Associate the lessons to the groups

This document, with the lessons for everyone included, should probably be a spreadsheet. You will want a row for each lesson name showing the user group or groups who need that lesson, the number of learners in each group, their location or locations, any time requirements for delivery (more on this below), and any other information that you capture that could influence your decisions downstream about how to best deliver the necessary training to each group.

To arrive at this, you might find it helpful to first organize the information by user group during your research stage. After all, you don't know all of the lessons that will be needed until you finish analyzing each group's needs. But you also need the information organized by lesson, not by group, so that you can see the common needs across multiple groups.

One way to do this would be to first build a spreadsheet with the raw data organized by user group, and then create a new sheet referencing that data but organized by lesson. This way, as changes occur or as you refine your data with new information, you can make those changes where it makes sense – in the spreadsheet organized by user group – and then refresh the second spreadsheet, the one organized by lesson, to include the new data.

Analyze delivery needs

Once you have a spreadsheet showing who needs what content, you can analyze how to deliver that content optimally, both in terms of effectiveness and in terms of efficiency. Sometimes these two values will be in tension with each other, and you will need to make decisions based on the budget and on the strategic importance of a particular group or subject.

Your analysis should include the factors below:

Geography

Where are the learners physically located? Are they all in one office, or spread over dozens or hundreds of locations around the country or around the world?

Generally speaking, the more distributed the geography, the more savings likely to be found in distance learning, because the travel costs of sending an army of instructors out to all those locations, plus the costs of setting up physical classrooms and materials in each, will tend to be high.

The key variable is not how far apart the offices are, but how many of them there are. Your company could have one office in North America and another in Asia, but the distance between the two is not much of a cost factor. On the other hand, if you have fifty small branch offices across one large state or province, the costs associated with instructor-led training could be enormous.

Numbers of learners

There are two elements involved here. How many learners are there for a given lesson, in total, and how many are there in each location? You can see that this is related to the geography criterion: if you have 1,000 people who need to learn a lesson, whether you go for instructor-led learning or perhaps an online lesson will depend, in part, on how many of those people are located in the same place or small number of places.

If they are in 1,000 different locations, go with distance learning. If they're all in the main office, you might still go with online learning, but you could also decide to do classroom instruction if that will be more effective for that combination of material and learners.

Generally speaking, the more learners there are for a given lesson, the more it makes sense economically to go with online or other learning that doesn't require that fleet of instructors and wired classrooms. It costs more to develop online learning, on a per-development-hour basis, but you more than recoup these higher development costs with far, far lower delivery costs.

For example, say that in your organization, training development of ILT (instructor-led training) takes an average of 30 development hours for each instructional hour. And say that online instruction takes four times as long in the development phase, for a ratio of 120 development hours for each instructional hour.

On the face of it, online learning looks four times as expensive. But if that learning gets delivered to 500 learners at little to no delivery cost, whereas ILT requires a live instructor, a physical classroom, printed materials, computers, and a training database to use for practice that may require many hours of custom development, suddenly online learning begins to look a lot cheaper. If you have ten students in each class, you need no fewer than 50 ILT classes to deliver the training. That's a lot of instructors and classrooms.

True, if you have an exceptionally open-ended timeframe in which training can take place, and you can use the same classroom over and over, with only one instructor, until all 50 classes happen, that saves on some of the delivery costs of ILT. You would only need to wire one classroom. But you would still be paying the instructor for each of those 50 class hours, and you would still need the materials and the training database.

One other reason why online learning saves on the delivery end actually has to do with development, not delivery. That's because you can sometimes cover the material in fewer delivery hours when the learners are self-directed. Think of all the times in school when you were bored because one or a few students didn't get the material as fast as others; the entire class had to go slower as a result. So a three-hour ILT class might take only two hours, or less, for many of the online learners to get through. When they get through the lesson faster, with mastery, they get back to work faster. And that's a real cost savings.

Languages

You may need to translate and/or localize your training lessons, whether your company operates across borders or even within one country. It depends on the languages understood by the learners.

If you need to conduct training in more than one language, you will not only need to translate your materials, whether delivered as ILT or online, and you may also need to hire instructors to deliver ILT in the required target languages.

If most of the training will be in one language, with a relatively small number of learners requiring training in another language, you may be able to keep costs down by carefully scheduling the extra instructors to minimize their downtime between classes.

Schedules

The schedule most on the critical path for your training project is the overall project implementation schedule. With few exceptions, you need to have training delivery completed in time for the cutover to the new system. Yes, it's sometimes possible that a few non-key groups can get their training after that, but generally speaking, training has to be over before implementation takes place, and ideally, it is over just before then, so that the learners don't have time to forget what they have learned.

Generally speaking, the last thing you want is for your training plan to drive the dates for the overall project, because that means that you are now in everyone's crosshairs as the critical path of the overall project. If you are late, the overall project will be late. Not a healthy place to be, if you can avoid it.

Projects do sometimes have unrealistic schedules, and it's conceivable that you may face the political question of how to present your realistic schedule when everybody else is presenting unrealistic ones. Armed with real data that you have analyzed in forming this training plan, you can, hopefully, point out that if there are 1000 users to train, and Operations will only allow 50 of them off the floor at one time for classes, then this means that you will need 20 separate class sessions. And even that is assuming that you have five classrooms to use, with ten learners in each. If you don't, then simple math and the laws of physics dictate that it will take longer to get everyone through the training.

Like many (but not all) project management problems, additional budget could help solve this one. If, for example, you can build more classrooms and hire more instructors, you can have more classes going on simultaneously.

But if you can't, it's both okay and necessary to show that you know what you're talking about in your part of the overall project by showing the possible timelines given the current setup. Using this information, the overall project managers can make the necessary adjustments to the overall project plan, whether in terms of budget, schedule, or resource allocations.

In addition to the overall project schedule, you also need to analyze the work schedule of the people you need to train. Do they all work the day shift? If there are 10 people who need a lesson, all in one office, it sounds like one class – but not if those ten people are spread over three shifts, and you can only take one out of three workers off the floor for training at any one given time.

Also, since there is real work that needs to get done even while the training project is underway, you need to be aware of the overall work schedule for each group of users. If you are training retail employees, for example, it's likely that the holiday season will be off-limits to you for scheduling any training sessions.

Create a budget

Once you have analyzed the training needs and come up with a defensible training plan to meet them, you can assign dollar values to the plan components.

You've identified all the lessons, and all the groups of learners who need them. You've identified how you're going to deliver each piece of the training to each group of learners.

Direct costs

For each lesson, estimate the development time required (see chapter 9 on how to do this), estimate the delivery costs (primarily for ILT), and add them up. These are your direct costs.

About delivery costs for ILT: you can calculate the number of instructors, sets of materials, network setup needed, etc. all from the number of students that you have identified. Depending on the implementation schedule – that is, if you can spread out the training over time – you can get by with fewer classrooms and instructors; if the window for training is more compressed, you'll need to run more classes simultaneously, and therefore you'll need more classrooms and instructors, as well as more system resources for training purposes.

Indirect costs

In addition to these direct costs, you might also need to add indirect costs in some organizations, such as management time, administrative support, materials costs, and the like.

Adjust the budget to needs and constraints

This preliminary budget should be based on your analysis of the training needs and your professional opinion as to how to best meet them. But training does not occur in a vacuum or in a perfect business world, and you will almost certainly need to make some adjustments to your preferred plan based on business needs and constraints.

It's a very good idea to work through all the scenarios that you can think of before you go to get your manager's approval. If, for example, the boss says you need to get it done with 10% less, the atmosphere in the room will be considerably different if you can pull out an alternative budget that meets that requirement – with the resulting impacts also clearly laid out, so that the decision will be an informed one.

Thus, when you take the numbers to your executive and say, "here's what I recommend," you can show why. If the required budget isn't available, you can then consider the options together, such as reducing the duration (with the ensuing potential reduction in effectiveness), spreading out the schedule so you can stay in-house instead of renting facilities, etc. In some organizations, training budgets come from the affected departments, while in others it comes from the training department, and in some cases (such as implementation of a new system) it comes from the budget for that overall project.

Other budget considerations

It's unlikely that you will always be working on one and only one training project. So one additional budget consideration that you need to keep in mind is resource availability. Why? Because few organizations can afford to staff at a level to handle the maximum peak of the required work over the course of the year.

Every department has peaks and valleys in its workload. Except for the most critical of training functions, where the success of the training program is literally a matter of life and death – think pilot training, or training for operators of nuclear facilities – it just doesn't make economic sense to staff at 100% of the peak needs.

Most organizations will choose to staff at somewhere around 70-80% of their peak needs, assuming that the peaks are relatively infrequent. This means that sometimes there will be a bit of slack in the schedule, time that your training group can use for professional development, for team-building, for long-term projects, for learning new technologies, and the like.

And it also means that there will be times when there isn't enough time in the work schedule to assign 100% of your trainers' time to a given project, because they may have to work on more than one project at a time.

Not an ideal situation, but a very realistic and frequent one in the business world, and as a manager, you need to be able to plan for this. More information on how to estimate projects with this sort of complexity in mind is in chapter 9. For the purpose of this section on budgeting, it's enough for now to know that resource availability will have an impact on the budget – and the available budget will have an impact on the resources that you can use for any given project.

Approve or obtain approvals

Whose approval you need for a given project depends on the organization and project. If you are a profit center, where the client is paying for the training, you might need the approval (or just FYI) of your own manager, plus the overall project manager, plus the client.

If you are a cost center, meaning that the training is provided at no cost to the client or that the training is internal within your organization, you will likely need the approval of your manager and the manager of the group whose internal budget will be charged.

It's crucial that you identify the necessary approvers in advance, so that you do not end up working on a project that does not have all the necessary signoffs. It sometimes makes business sense to start a project before the dotted line gets signed, but there is obvious risk involved. Even with all the good faith in the world, the client may decide not to go ahead with the training or, at least, not with the program that you have planned. That's not something you want to happen mid-project.

It's also sometimes necessary to move up the approval chain to make sure that you have a *binding* approval. Not everyone has authority at every budget level, and depending on the scope of the project, you may need executive approval, not just a manager's direct approval.

Just as in contracts, you want to make sure that the person signing, or in this case signing off, is an authorized signer!

Chapter 4
Training development

If you need to develop your own material, then you build it backwards. For each lesson, start with the end objective – what it is that the people need to start doing as a result of taking this lesson. Remember, training is not about knowledge. That would be education. Training is about behaviors.

Build on a straight line

Then build your content on as straight a line as you can toward that goal of what people need to start doing after they complete the lessons in the training program. The units in a training program are called lessons, and your job is to create the right lessons, only the necessary lessons, and create them well, so that the right stuff gets learned.

Make the training task-based

Organizing training around the system is the wrong way to go; it's like reading a reference manual aloud to someone. Not an effective method, especially for tasks that go across menus and multi-step tasks. And people will tune out after a few minutes, because there is no way to readily justify why they need to know what's in the File menu. What they need to know is how to get their job done the right way using the new system.

So make your training task-based. To do this, refer to your needs analysis. That should pretty much list the tasks that users need to be trained to do. And so your training development should follow that list directly. If you find your training program beginning to veer off in another direction, bring it back to what your training needs analysis showed you need to train. The only exception would be if you need to update the needs analysis itself due to changed or previously unknown conditions.

What does task-based training mean? It means that instead of training system functions, you train users to perform tasks. Some of those tasks, perhaps even most all of them, include making use of the system. The difference is one of perspective: tasks are what people actually do in their jobs. Nobody's job is to move the cursor around on a screen and click on buttons, so it makes no sense to organize training around which buttons appear on which screen. What makes sense is to understand the scenarios in which users go through various screens in the system to get something done. That scenario is essentially the outline of your task-based lesson.

Train common tasks, not exceptions

Training often doesn't even cover all of the identified tasks. This is for two reasons. First, economy. If you have two days for a course, you can only fit in two days' worth of material. The rest will have to be left for the documentation in any case, no matter how fast you can talk. For this reason and more, it's often a good practice to train people in class to look things up in the documentation or online help so that they will know how to do this once they're back in the field – and so that they will know that they *can* do this back in the field.

The second reason is pedagogic. If you were to try to train every task (assuming that there are many), people will remember only selectively (especially the lessons taught at the beginning and at the end of the course, at the expense of the middle lessons), in what psychologists call the primary-recency effect. That is, people remember more of what was at the beginning and at the end, and less of what was in the middle. So by including less important or less frequently performed tasks, you will *ensure* that some of the important and frequent ones will not be remembered. That's bad news.

So when you develop training, order the lessons from common tasks to rare, and from simple to complex. Then, like an editor with a news story, chop with a meat cleaver at the point where you can't fit any more. As long as the order is correct (just as later paragraphs in a news story are of descending importance), you'll be okay. In fact, you'll be more than okay: you will have ensured that your training program covers the most important, most commonly-performed tasks. That's good news!

It's good news because the purpose of most training programs is to get the users up and running so they can perform basic tasks. Full information on all the glorious features of your system, along with unimportant tasks and variants of the main tasks, go in the user guides or help.

Why? Imagine a system with 12 different ways to search for a customer record. In class, you teach the common ones – probably name and phone number – and leave the other 10 to the doc or online help. If you dragged your students through all 12 ways in class, you'd bore them immensely, and you would also make it likely that they would forget the first 2 ways (the important, common ones). Instead, identify the commonly used and important stuff, and teach – *in the class* – how to look up the rest in the reference materials.

Focus on the most common activities (and leave exception handling to the documentation). Leave out anything nice to have if it isn't necessary in getting people to the behaviors you need from them. Be rigorous about this: if you include unnecessary lessons, you're wasting your company's or your customer's money. Add up the hourly costs of all the people in all of those unnecessary lessons, and not only will you endanger the success of your current training project, you may put future ones at risk, too, because you will have earned the reputation of being costly and inefficient.

The exception to this rule about training only common tasks and not exceptions is when the exception handling is so vitally important that it must be trained. For example, if you are training airline pilots, it's obviously insufficient to train only how to take off normally, how to coast along on autopilot, and how to land normally, which is what pilots do most of the time. You have to train for the very unlikely, but highly dangerous, unusual situations. What happens when an engine falls off the airplane? What happens if the landing gear doesn't deploy? Most pilots (and passengers!), thankfully, will never experience either situation, yet all pilots must be trained to deal with such unlikely situations.

In a corporate context, where the drama of in-flight emergencies does not occur, there could still be some groups for whom exception training is necessary. Generally, the exceptions do not have to be part of everyone's training program. Often, supervisors or support staff can train on the exceptions, and regular users can simply be trained to refer to the experts as needed.

Include necessary prerequisites

Now, having said that you should build your content on a straight line to your actual learning objectives, there may be some lessons that depend on prerequisites. In this case, it is both okay and necessary to include lessons that cover building blocks or prerequisite knowledge, often concepts that are both new and necessary to be able to start doing that new behavior correctly.

Just remember your Prime Directive, as they used to say on Star Trek. Keep your eyes on getting your students to the defined goal. Anything else is superfluous, and superfluous is a bad thing in training: if you mix necessary and unimportant material in your training program, the students will naturally come away thinking that the unimportant stuff that you thought added spice was actually the real lesson.

Structuring your training lessons

Each lesson should have the structure outlined below:

Introduction

Here's where you *briefly* explain what the lesson is about, putting it in the context of the workflow.

Lesson Objective

In a sentence or two, describe what *exactly* the students will learn to do in this lesson. Don't be general, don't tell stories, and don't talk about what prompted you to create this lesson. Instead, list the actual task or tasks that the students will be able to perform as a result of taking this lesson.

Why You Need to Know

This is crucial, because it forces you to justify the lesson content to the users – and to yourself. If you can't think of a reason for a lesson, chances are you need to rework – or trash – the lesson. You have to *explicitly* tell the students why they need to bother giving this lesson their time and attention. And no, the reason is not because their boss said so. The reason must be why they need to know how to do this task or set of tasks *in the context of their work.*

Adult learners need to know why they should care. They've got a zillion things to do back at their desks, and you are taking up their time. Show them at the start of the lesson that you are aware of this, and justify the importance of the lesson in terms that will make a difference in their work.

For example: "This lesson shows you how to encrypt your emails. You need to know this so you can avoid exposing the company's trade secrets on our new product when you communicate with our remote plant."

You'll find that setting this down in words will focus you on what the students actually need to learn in order to accomplish their business tasks with your software or whatever, as opposed to what the software's glorious features are or what you, the author of the lesson, happen to know about the system.

If you don't directly tie your lesson to a benefit (namely, what paying attention for the next 50 minutes will get them), the students will rightly tune out.

Tasks

These are the heart of the lesson. Once you've motivated the learners by showing them that you understand why they need to know what's in this lesson, it's time to get to the actual tasks to be trained.

In a systems training context, this means one or more tasks, some or all of which employ the system (though some can also be offline tasks). For each task, give the procedures to follow, demonstrate the task, and have the students follow.

Exercises

If tasks are the heart of the lesson, exercises are the heart of the learning. You've explained, you've demonstrated, the students have followed along with you. Now it's time for them to do exercises on their own. In these exercises, you're not walking them through the task anymore. Instead, you're walking around the room (assuming classroom delivery) and helping those who need it.

The purpose of exercises, which should always be hands-on, if at all possible (virtually, if not actually), is for students to practice on their own what they have learned in the lesson. It is in this hands-on application of knowledge that learning takes place, and if your schedule requires that you trim your carefully thought-out training program, you will usually be better off including fewer lessons with more hands-on exercises than trying to cram in more lessons without that hands-on exercise component.

So, within each lesson, make the learning as hands-on as you possibly can. If you're teaching a system, *use* the system (in simulation mode, if necessary). The more time that learners' hands are on keyboards or system controls or whatever, and the less time spent in frontal lectures by an instructor, the better the learning in almost all cases.

Remember, if it's training, it shouldn't be a lecture. People learn by doing.

Review or Quiz

Use either a review or an informal quiz to reinforce and measure learning. A review need not be at the end of every lesson. In my experience, reviews work better just after breaks. People come back from lunch or whatever and the morning's lessons may be jumbled together in their minds. One great way to untangle that knowledge is to review the material using humor and without embarrassing anyone. How can you do this? An example is to use slides or handouts with questions about the material learned. Make it multiple-choice, and make the answer totally obvious…and the wrong answers funny.

The idea is not to make it hard to see which answer is correct; the idea is to make it utterly obvious, and to do this in an entertaining and memorable way.

I'm reminded of the test I took to get my first driver's license. I'm sure they didn't intend for it to be funny in this way, but it was. One of the questions was something like this:

You arrive at an intersection where there is an eight-sided, red sign with white lettering that says STOP. What should you do?

- *Continue through the intersection without slowing down.*

- *Slow down, then proceed through the intersection without looking.*

- *Increase your speed as you proceed through the intersection.*

- *Come to a full and complete stop. Look in all directions to determine when it is safe to proceed, and when it is, proceed slowly and with caution through the intersection.*

I took that test over 30 years ago, and still remember it (whether or not this was intentional on the part of the test author). Try to make your training that memorable!

Instructor Guides

In some cases, where you have a full-blown training program taught by various instructors, or when the training developer will not be the person delivering the training, you may need to create an Instructor Guide. Formats for these guides can vary. Some include replicas of the student materials, along with additional information. That can be a burdensome document to create and keep in sync with the student workbooks. It is often easier to leave out the replication and instead include in the Instructor Guide only the extra information an instructor needs to teach the lesson effectively.

What does this information include? Explain the business context enveloping the lesson, list likely student questions or common problems, along with the solutions, and provide the answers to the exercises and the review. Also include suggested timing for the lessons, setup information, and examples to use during class.

A good instructor guide can help avoid the problem where the instructional designer (which in this case is you or someone on your team) sloppily relies on the instructor to "fill in the gaps." What if the instructor doesn't know?

Presentations

Create presentations as visual aids for the instructor to use. Mind, a presentation is NOT training – its purpose is as a visual aid, especially when there is conceptual material that requires explanation, and to illustrate points in the lesson.

And when you use a presentation in a lesson, please don't turn your back on the learners and read the text on the slide to them! You should know the material well enough to talk to the points made without reading what they can plainly see themselves.

Chapter 5
Training delivery

As described in chapter 3, after you analyze who needs what in terms of training content, lesson by lesson and course by course, you've got to consider how to deliver this training to the masses. Or, if your entire training audience consists of seven people, *that's* what you need to consider. Refer back to your spreadsheet with the numbers of each kind of person and location. Use this and the other factors there to decide what makes sense for training delivery.

Choose a delivery method: instructor-led or online

The two primary methods of delivering training are ILT – instructor-led training (also called classroom training), and what used to be called CBT – computer-based training or WBT – web-based training, now often called online learning. These days, "learning" is more in fashion than "training," because it focuses on the person doing the learning and not on what is being learned, but to my mind, this is not terribly important in the context of creating and managing a training program.

When you develop a training program, as detailed in the previous chapter, you are already focusing on the drilled-down needs of each identifiable group with its individual characteristics, and then creating lessons to meet those needs.

But while the centrality of the learners is obvious in this process, in most business and organizational settings, it's still going to be primarily about what they need to learn more than who they are as learners.

All this to say that the terminology of the training industry changes, and that different practitioners will use different terms for the same things. Not to worry.

Back to the question of ILT or online learning:

If you've got more than several hundred people taking a course, especially if they're spread out geographically, you can save a bundle on travel and classroom logistical expenses if you can sensibly deliver part or all of the training over the web. The more people who need the course, the more likely that it will be worth it to spend up to five times as much on development in order to save on delivery. (Numbers vary, but typical classroom system training takes about 25-30 hours of development for each delivery hour, while e-learning can be five or more times that. On the other hand, not only do you save on travel with e-learning, but it usually goes about 30% faster than classroom learning, as described in chapter 3.)

When the training needs to be completed is not only an input into the decisions on delivery methods, but also into the decisions on development. For example, if there's a big rush, you might need to develop several stages of training, with only the most pressing material being covered in stage one, or combine web learning with instructor-led in what is called blended learning. You might also pilot material that will later get rolled out into a full online learning program by training pilot users in a first class.

Classroom training: instructor-led

If you go the classroom route, you need to meticulously plan the logistics. Some organizations have state-of-the-art training facilities. Many don't, and even those that do often do not have the facilities in place for a full-scale conversion training program where everyone needs to be trained on a new system. Most corporate training facilities are instead designed, and properly so, for new hire and refresher training, where small groups of learners take part – not the whole company.

To determine whether you have the training facilities you will need for your training program, you'll need to compare them with your delivery needs as shown in your training needs analysis spreadsheet. Sometimes delivery schedule requirements can be renegotiated a bit when the facilities just don't allow two classes to happen in the same room at the same time; other times, the demands are driven by factors that can't be changed.

If you don't have enough classrooms to deliver the classes you need when you need them, you can rent external facilities or, if it makes economic sense, you can create new temporary classrooms to get past a schedule bulge. Conference rooms often get converted temporarily into classrooms for just this reason.

Scheduling is very complex, especially if you can't close down a whole department during class time and take all their people away from their regular work at the same time. If you have to train people at the end of their regular work day, you've got to deal with them being tired and less receptive – meaning that your material has to be that much better!

If you have networks and whatnot to set up for your classrooms, you'll need to see to that. Same with printing of materials – make sure the right materials arrive to the right classroom before the class starts. Scheduling the instructors is also something you'll need to do; if not all instructors can teach all courses, you've got to schedule accordingly. By the way, you'll need to identify and train the instructors.

Especially in a classroom training rollout, you must stay on top of all these logistical details, using project management software and methodology. Otherwise, your beautiful training materials won't find their way to the instructors and students in the classroom at the right time in the right place, and the system won't be there for them to use in their learning.

Online learning

If you go the e-learning route (and possibly also if you do go with classroom learning), your next decision – even though this section is on training delivery – is whether to develop in-house or to use a vendor.

If you are doing a one-off project and don't have a bunch of time on your hands to learn how to do e-learning, you're better off outsourcing. If you do, make sure you manage the process closely with your vendor to make sure that the content that gets created is to your standard and is delivered on time. Do not expect that magic will happen!

Unless your subject matter requires it, skip the bells and whistles that the vendor may want to push on you. Focus on content, and make sure this is clear to the vendor. Training content, whether online or printed, should be a step or two above downright ugly, but for most training needs, functional is the way to go. Of course, there are exceptions to every rule: if you are training fashion designers, that's a crowd with different expectations and, most probably, learning needs, than the usual bunch.

In terms of delivery options, the buzzword for the last few years has been blended learning, meaning a combination of e-learning and classroom learning. For example, if the whole organization of several thousand employees spread over two dozen locations needs to take your Intro to Info Security lesson, make that one a lesson delivered through e-learning. Then you can follow up with the specifics of what each group needs in the classroom.

Set the tone: fun exploration

The best learning in classes I've taken and classes I've taught happened when the instructor set a tone of fun exploration – that is, if the students picked up on it and ran with it.

This is the magic that you have to try to create in a class, and you can only do it through a combination of:

- mastery of the subject

- a sympathetic understanding of the students and the issues that they face in their work environment, including the natural fear of change

- a dedicated effort to make even dreary subjects as interesting as possible

- making the students the ones in charge of the learning through lots of hands-on exercises and simulations, and precious little lecturing.

Training delivery management

If yours is a large project, get management buy-in from the start and continuously. It will take a significant budget no matter how you do it, and the training project will be highly visible throughout your company. So make sure you get a clear understanding of what your company wants to accomplish with this program, so that you can build your objectives and choose among the options accordingly.

Chapter 6
Training evaluation

The Kirkpatrick model

Probably the most commonly used model to measure success of training is by Donald Kirkpatrick. That model has four levels. They go something like this:

Level one – reaction

At this level, all you are measuring is the reaction of the students to the course, or in other words, whether the students *liked* the course.

This is commonly measured by a questionnaire, aka a "smile sheet," since typically scores are falsely high. It doesn't tell you much. At the end of a course, students want to get out of the room, and it's just easier to quickly check all 10s than to seriously evaluate the course. And most smile sheets don't allow or encourage any in-depth evaluation, just 1-to-5 or 1-to-10 scales to check off.

Still, it's better to get higher evaluations than lower ones, even at level one of the model, because while a high score does not necessarily indicate high quality, if someone does actually give you a low score on a level-one evaluation, that can be a sign that something is seriously wrong with your course or instructor.

Level two – learning

At level two, you try to ascertain whether the students actually learned anything, or more specifically, whether they learned what you wanted them to learn. Unlike level one, this level measures what the students learn, as measured by a pre- and post-test, and is therefore a better measure than a level one smile sheet. Many trainers are very pleased when the scores improve from pre- to post-, but in most cases this is still an incomplete measure of a course's success.

A low score can reflect a variety of causes – for example, if they don't remember much of what you taught them, this might be because your teaching was at fault. But it might also be because the content was not what they needed. Or maybe the room was noisy. Or perhaps there was missing prerequisite knowledge. Or a language/localization issue. Or business distractions that kept the students from focusing on the course.

Conversely, a high score still doesn't tell you that your course has the value you hope it does. All it tells you is that the students can spit back at you what you gave them. Yes, in theory the pre- and post-test should be directly related to the learning objective for the course. But the ability to regurgitate does not necessarily indicate true acquisition of knowledge.

Level three – behavior

Level three asks if the students are able to *apply* what they learned on the job through changed behavior.

Now we're getting to the interesting part. In contrast to levels one and two, success on this level means that you are teaching what you intended to teach, and that it's getting across, and that it's being used on the job.

Of course, it's also a lot harder to measure. A quick and dirty method would be to *ask* the students if their behavior will change or has changed, but their answers may or may not be entirely reliable. A more scientific approach would include empirical observation, but many corporations don't have the time or budget resources for this.

A good level three evaluation can tell you whether the students have changed their behavior back on the job. But what it can't tell you is what you most want to know: did your training program not only make a difference, but did it make the *right* difference? Did it solve the business or organizational problem that it was supposed to solve? For that, you need to evaluate on level four.

Level four – results

At level four, you evaluate whether the training has had an impact on the bottom line. Hopefully, that impact will be positive.

This is clearly the hardest to measure, even though it is the question that you or your boss most want to have answered. If level one measures satisfaction of the students with the training, and level two measures whether they learned what you wanted them to learn, and level three measures whether they applied this learning back on the job, only level four measures whether all this was worth the cost. Did it make a difference? Were there fewer mistakes made? Were the forms processed faster? Did customer hold times on the phone decrease? Were sales goals achieved?

Like in level three, possibly the closest you can get to measuring this without devoting inordinate amounts of time is to ask the students, their bosses, or other appropriate people in the organization who may have measures in place that you can hitch a ride on. Other ways might include measurements of productivity: were more calls handled because reps knew the system better?

But these also have to control for other factors – for example, perhaps the students began working on faster PCs during the period being measured, or perhaps workforce fluctuations (vacations, illness, retirements, etc.) or seasonal variations in workload meant that the individual or team workload was greater or smaller, or whatever.

So, even in level four, the work of measuring and evaluating the impact of training can still be challenging. Nonetheless, being able to measure and demonstrate the effectiveness – and therefore the *cost-effectiveness* – of your training programs is absolutely crucial. Without it, you are simply flying blind, and your training group will be subject to the cost-cutting whims of management the next time expense reductions are needed.

Being able to show the value of your team's work is really important!

How to create evaluation questionnaires

Not every organization and situation can allow for a full-blown training evaluation program on all four levels. So how can you make the most out of the evaluation options open to you?

One approach, especially in a lean organization or when the students are your company's customers and not part of your organization, is to try to collapse levels two through four down into your otherwise level-one questionnaire. On your questionnaires, include questions on every aspect of your class that you can think of, and don't be afraid to give students a multi-page questionnaire for even a one-day course.

Make your questions count. Don't ask, "Was the instructor good?" Ask instead:

- Did the instructor know the material?
- Was the instructor prepared?
- Did the instructor answer your questions well?
- How engaging was the instructor?
- What suggestions would you offer the instructor for the next class?

and so on. Write detailed questions about the instructor, the materials, the venue, the timing, the coffee, and every other aspect of your course. Only in these details will you get any information that you can actually use to improve your course. Balance quick-answer questions (the ones with 1-5 ratings) with word questions that require free text answers.

If you stick to a one-pager with generalities, you'll get "good" (remember the smile sheets) simply because it's easier for the student to finish quicker that way and leave the room. A useful questionnaire is probably at least three pages, and includes questions that try to measure at least the students' *opinions* about level three and four success, even if you can't actually go out and measure those empirically. After every course, tabulate the scores for each question to see if there are any significant deviations from the usual good-to-very-good rating. Track these ratings by course and by instructor.

Remember to keep your training – whatever the subject – as hands-on as possible. This will help you move toward level-four success, which means that your training has a real and positive impact. If you train theoretically, you may get good level one or two scores, but you won't accomplish much. So if you have to choose between more hands-on exercises and covering all the material, go for the exercises. It is better to successfully train the most important subjects than to fail by trying to cover them all badly. You can put the extra material in a user guide or help for future reference.

Communicate the evaluations

Whatever the results of the evaluation are, you should communicate them to your team, to the other stakeholders, and possibly to a wider audience as well.

Yes, *whatever the results*. If a program hasn't worked, people will know. Now, you can either have them assume that the failure was your fault, or you can figure out what the problems were and talk about them. If the budget was tight, if the timeline meant that you had to develop training before the new system was ready, if you had to use more distance learning than would have been optimal because of the learners' geographic distribution, these all need to be pointed out.

Most of the time, though, you will succeed. And since people do have something better to do with their time than read your reports, you can and should summarize the key points. Perhaps, in a challenging project, the fact that you got it *done*, even if imperfectly, is the main point. If so, it's entirely legitimate to feature this in your report: "We delivered 37 different courses to 2,490 students in 5 locations, making sure that at least 80% of all students passed the first time, even though the course had to be developed before the system was ready." That sure beats "20% of the students failed our courses," and it sure as all heck beats a rumor mill about one-fifth of the students failing. You, as the communicator in this operation, need to communicate! Take stock of the raw data from your evaluations, draw your conclusions, and communicate them so that next time will be even better.

You can feel legitimate about communicating your group's successes, because you will be able to demonstrate those successes, using the data from the student evaluations that you have analyzed. And a nice way to do this without being self-aggrandizing is to publicly thank each of the stakeholders involved for their role in the success instead of taking any credit yourself. By praising others, you show that your team's work is worthy of praise. And that reflects doubly nicely on you.

So your email to the relevant business group managers, to the SMEs and their managers, to your team and your manager, and to any other people who helped make the training happen, briefly summarizes the successful training that just happened and thanks each of them, and especially your training developers and delivery specialists, for their good work.

Thanking others makes everyone feel good, and it makes you feel good about your team's work.

Chapter 7
How to hire trainers

Trainers sometimes move up into management and need to hire other trainers. While they may have great training experience themselves, this doesn't always mean they know how to decide who would be a good choice for the team.

In other cases, the manager hiring a trainer is not a trainer, and doesn't necessarily know a whole lot about how to hire a trainer, or what makes a good one. So here is a brief guide on how to hire a trainer, for trainers who become managers and for non-trainer managers who are tasked with finding a new trainer for the team.

Establish the requirements

Whether you're a manager who doesn't know exactly what it is that trainers do, or an experienced trainer now in a management role, you need to find out or think about what it is a successful trainer should be able to do in your company before you start your search. How else will you know who meets your requirements?

Some suggestions for defining the job requirements are below.

Interview stakeholders

Talk to the outgoing trainer, if there is one, or other members of the training team, if any. Ask them what makes for a good trainer in your organization – which could be very different from the success criteria in another. If the conversation goes too far in the direction of personality – though this, too, can be useful information – try to steer it back into the realm of skills in a broad sense.

Find out what skills and tools the trainer needs, but this shouldn't be the focus. Any good trainer who knows one tool can pick up a similar one fast. The focus should be on how the work gets done in your company. What knowledge, skills, or characteristics make for success in discovering, or ferreting out, the required information in your context? Do they need to understand fiber optics, or clinical pharmacology, or robotics in automobile manufacturing? Do they need to be able to read and follow the flow of programming code, even if they're not themselves programmers? Do they need to be able to sell to a classroom of salespeople? Do they need to communicate with the engineers to get the information that somehow never makes it into the spec? Are there aspects of your company culture that they must be able to absorb in order to get the information they need to do their work? Do they have to be able to invent information for reviewers to correct, instead of waiting for experts to explain things to them?

You want to build a composite picture based on multiple interviews, with the trainer-to-be's peers, supervisors, SMEs, support, internal clients, etc. This process is likely to help you in your own quest to improve your group's relations with other departments. Even though you are not offering them veto power over your hiring process, imagine the effect you will produce by asking the engineers what qualities they think a trainer should have. They will see that you care about overall quality and the process required to achieve that quality, and that you are not caught up inside your own silo unaware of the rest of the company and its needs.

Consult with human resources

Talk to your HR or Recruiting department and get them to provide updated salary range information for trainers in your industry and geographic area. They can also be a big help in helping you define soft skills that your candidate should have.

Perhaps most important, in the legal environment of the United States, is the guidance HR can give you on how to ensure that your search is legal and ethical. It isn't hard to do such a search. But many managers make easily-prevented mistakes, even if they intended well. You are generally not allowed to discriminate in your hiring decisions on the basis of race, sex, religion, age, and various other criteria – nor should you. So don't ask a candidate how old they are, what their marital status is, or other irrelevant and probably illegal questions.

Beyond not saying improper words in an interview, you also need to establish fair hiring criteria; i.e. criteria that focus on the work to be done and not on the personal background of the candidates. See below regarding testing in the hiring process.

Define the business goal: why are you hiring?

If you're hiring a new trainer, you're committing your company to a major expense that will last a long time. So it behooves you to figure out what it is you need the trainer to be able to do.

From a business perspective – after all, you *are* a manager – figure out what you need the trainer to produce, and figure out what makes those training programs, or widgets, or whatever, a success for you in the context of your business.

For example, if you work in a software company – where in some cases the training group works hand-in-hand with development, or more likely, has to find ways to get the developers to devote time to giving them information and reviews of drafts at the same time that they're still busy fixing bugs so the software can go out the door on time – "interpersonal skills" on the part of a new trainer are not just fuzzy HR-speak, but something you really need the trainer to have. Otherwise, they won't be able to be flexible and creative in getting the developers to give them the time they need from them. The last thing you need is a trainer who gives up working with the engineers because it's a challenge to get their cooperation.

For another example, if your company is very process-oriented, you need to be cognizant of this characteristic when looking for trainers. Trainers who prefer a greater degree of independence might have a hard time fitting in. Conversely – and I think this happens more often – if you are a company focused more on getting the current project out the door than in adhering to what your company sees as cumbersome process, then you need someone who can roll with the punches when it comes time to drop the quality process and crank out the workbooks. In this scenario, you do not want to hire someone who can't handle the business necessity of shipping the training materials even when they are still imperfect.

Put the criteria together

Now it's time to sit down and put these all together. You might find it helpful to put your criteria into columns in a spreadsheet, and put the various candidates in rows, so you can compare one with another across the board. For each criterion, you can give a simple grade of 1 for strong, 0 for neutral, and -1 for weak. If you want to give extra weight to certain criteria, it's probably easier to do that at the end when you tally scores: simply build a formula that weighs various columns more than others.

Your spreadsheet might include criteria like these:

Training development skills

How well can this person create a lesson? You have three items to consider: the candidate's resume, the candidate's samples, and the results of a test you administer.

1. Resume – this is the trainer's calling card.

    a. Accuracy – is the resume perfectly accurate? There's really no reason why a trainer's resume should have mistakes of fact or writing errors. As a hiring manager, I was surprised how few resumes passed this simple screening device. But a trainer is responsible for producing accurate lessons. Trainers who can't produce an accurate resume are likely not to be worth your bother.

    b. Organization – is the resume organized well? Remember, trainers are supposed to organize information on the job. Whether a trainer can organize a resume so the information is clearly and logically presented is something for you to judge. If a 1- or 2-page resume doesn't flow, how will a training class that spans several days flow?

A Practical Guide

    c. Excitement – okay, resumes are business documents, not suspense novels. But training programs are also business documents, and if they're boring, they're not good. A good trainer's resume will tell a story. It will grab you (in a businesslike way) and say, "read this!"

2. Samples – it's accepted practice for trainers to bring a portfolio with samples of their best work to show you in an interview. Your job as a hiring manager is to evaluate the samples critically to see what they say about the trainer. During the interview, the trainer will likely pull the samples out, show them to you briefly, and put them away. That's okay – in some cases, due to confidentiality agreements with previous employers or clients, the trainer can do no more. But you can ask about the work that the trainer did, specifically, on the samples shown. Ask what the biggest challenge was in a particular assignment. Ask who the trainer worked with to produce the lesson or class or program – the SMEs, perhaps an editor, perhaps co-trainers. Ask what the trainer is most proud of in each sample.

    a. Accuracy – if the trainer allows this, give the samples to members of your team for them to analyze and evaluate while you continue the interview. Have them look for writing errors, but also have them look for logic errors or structural flaws. Based on what the trainer tells you about the purpose of the sample and its intended audience, evaluate how well the training document appears to achieve its stated goals. If the trainer makes an electronic copy available to you, have your team look for spelling or other errors.

b. Organization – how well are the samples organized? First, look at the portfolio of samples as a whole. Does it reflect good organization? Are the pieces thoughtfully chosen, and do they reflect the skills that you are looking for? Next, look at each sample. How did the trainer organize each of the samples? Does that organization make sense, given the purpose of the sample? If the sample is a lesson, is it structured around a system, which may indicate that the trainer simply took the information provided by a SME and formatted it, or is it structured around user tasks, which probably indicates that the trainer actively processed the information from SMEs and other sources and then reformulated it into an organizational structure that makes sense for a user?

3. The Test – as described below, this is a crucial part of any intelligent hiring process involving a trainer. As a manager, you need to know whether a candidate can produce what you need. And the best way to find this out is in a simulation in miniature of the actual work process, through a test where the trainer creates a small training lesson in conditions similar to those of your workplace.

    a. Accuracy – there are two kinds of accuracy you will be looking for. One is accuracy: is what the trainer says, in the context of the test, true? For example, if your test asks candidates to train the basic arithmetic functions of the Windows Calculator, did the trainer cover all of the functions (or document a conscious decision to cover only the main functions), describe them correctly, and teach them in an appropriate level of detail?

    b. Organization – you will want to evaluate the test to see how well the candidates organize the material they write. While of course you need to take test conditions into account, good trainers will show thought in organizing the mini-lesson you have them write, generally moving from common tasks to rare ones, and from simple ones to complex ones. What? The lesson isn't task-based at all? Depending on your test – which is another way of saying depending on the kind of work your group actually does – this may be cause for serious concern.

c. Excitement – finally, finally, you get a chance to see the candidates' ability to create a training lesson with the tools you need them to use on the job if hired, with no question of authenticity or claiming someone else's work as their own. Does it make you want to really learn about the Windows calculator? Is there thought and imagination in this lesson? What about graphics? Games? Simulations? (In the context of a test of reasonable duration, it's probably fine for the candidate to simply mark with placeholders where these would go, instead of developing them fully.) In short, once you've established accuracy, does the lesson engage you as a potential learner?

Work Experience and Skills

Similar experience may be less important than many employers believe. Too many job ads ask for candidates who, to have all the desired qualifications (often listed as requirements!), would have had to already been working at the company. So if you are a manufacturer of aerospace equipment, you do not have to limit your search to trainers who have previously done training on aerospace equipment.

What you may want to do, though, is assess here whether what a candidate has done in the past is similar enough to what you would need the candidate to do for you if hired. Perhaps they have trained other industrial or scientific hardware; if so, they already know what kinds of lessons are needed in a training program for equipment of another kind, and all they would need to learn is how to train your kind of equipment. On the other hand, a candidate who had never done training about hardware, but only web technologies, would not have similar experience to what you need, and you might well assign a value of -1 to such a candidate in this column.

Verbal communication skills

You're looking to hire a trainer, not a talk show host. But you need to know whether candidates can work well with other team members, with you, and with SMEs, and of course whether they have good presentation skills if they will be doing classroom training. Some trainers are able to communicate well with programmers or engineers on an ongoing basis to get the information they need without wasting the SMEs' time. But not all are able to do this well – and some are able to communicate rather too well, and will drive the engineers crazy with their chitchat.

Some nervousness in an interview setting is natural; if you interview enough people over time, you will likely be able to quickly get a feel for a trainer's verbal communication skills. If a trainer seems shy at first and then opens up when you ask about their work samples, you'll see soon enough that they have a passion for their work and communicating about it.

Detective skills and persistence

Some trainers are happy to regurgitate the low-hanging fruit they are served in the form of information. They're satisfied with copying from use cases or specs directly into a student workbook without checking how things actually work themselves, or reading the software code itself, or spending quality time with the SMEs to make sure they have covered all the necessary material.

You need to measure, as best as you can, how likely a trainer is to be a bloodhound when necessary to get the facts. The way to ascertain this is in the interview. Ask the candidates to tell you about how they go about getting information; drill down in one or more of the samples and ask specifically about a time when the information was not readily available: how did they get what they needed? If the answer is, "well, the SME never had time for me," without further explanation of the heroic efforts undertaken by the trainer and the trainer's manager to work with the SME to extract the knowledge without impinging upon the SME's own tight development schedule, then you may have a problem.

Technical aptitude

Simply put, you want to assess how technical a trainer is if your group does technical training. Of course, different jobs and companies will need different levels of technical aptitude in a trainer. But measuring, to the extent that you are able, the knowledge and ability of training candidates may well pay off down the line when things get rough in a project. The trainer who can figure stuff out without running to the SME will deliver a training package on time even in a pressured project or be able to figure out and solve technical issues in a remote classroom so that the lesson can go on. A trainer who can't do that may turn in a package that is incomplete, inaccurate, or superficial, or be helpless if everything doesn't work exactly right out in the classroom.

Understands audience

While this may be hard for you to assess, it can be helpful to think about whether the trainer has shown, or can describe, an understanding of what the audience for the sample lesson needed and how the trainer worked to address those needs.

You can get an idea about how much a trainer understands various audiences by asking about the projects in the sample portfolio, focusing on who they were written for. If the answer is a generality – something like, "well, everybody" – that is a very different answer than "this particular lesson was written for customer service representatives in call centers, who are evaluated on how quickly they can handle a call from start to finish." Trainers who can answer with that kind of detail show that they have done their homework; they have taken the time to go out in the field, or at least ask someone who has, to get an understanding of their intended audience. When they teach their classes, they also learn from their students about their work, and incorporate that knowledge in future lessons.

Graphics and formatting skills

In some organizations, this may not be important. Large operations may have dedicated graphic artists, book designers, and all the rest to handle the visual side of things. But in many companies, the trainers are responsible for all aspects of their publications. So trainers who have at least some graphics and formatting skills may be a plus for you, or they may even be an absolute necessity.

To assess these skills, start with the trainer's resume, where software tools will almost certainly be listed. Ask, or have one of your team ask (if they know the tool better than you do), about how the trainer has used the tool, and some specifics about the tool to assess whether the trainer has basic, advanced, or pro levels of ability with the tool. Next, look at the samples to see how the trainer has used the tool, and ask about the decisions and issues the trainer faced in creating the sample. Finally, you can include elements of graphics and formatting in the test you give the candidates.

Personal Qualities

These are largely intangible and hard to quantify. To some extent, if you notice anything in these areas, it's likely to be on the negative side, though positives may present themselves as well.

1. Honest – you may be able to get a picture of candidates' honesty by asking them about their former or current team members, by looking in the document properties of their resumes and samples to see if someone else originally authored them, and especially, without fail, by checking references.

2. Flexible – trainers need to react well to changing project conditions. To try to find out whether a candidate is flexible, use the "tell me about a time when…" question in the interview. Formulate your questions around times of difficulty to find out how the trainer handled them. If the answer is that rules are rules, and there was just no way this trainer was going to turn in work for a rush project that wasn't on the six-month plan, that could be a large red flag in some organizations.

3. Team player – engineers can sometimes be given slack in the area of relating to fellow humans if their expertise is sufficiently great to make their boorishness tolerable. Trainers seldom have that luxury. You want to know if a trainer can work with others. This doesn't mean that the whole team has to go out

bowling together every week. But the nature of training requires working with people, both when developing a training program and when delivering it. Try having the candidates interview informally with members of your team. When you're out of the room, some of the pressure and nervousness that are a natural part of interviewing may be lessened, and your team members can help you assess whether a candidate is a team player.

4. Works independently – perhaps this is the flip side of being a team player. Good trainers also need to be able to close the virtual door of their cubicles and crank out the training materials. They need to be able to track down elusive information without anybody telling them that this is what they need to do. They need to take initiative – and you need to allow them to do this and support them when they do – to get their work done. Perhaps the best way to gauge this is in the interview, again using the "tell me about a time when…" question, aiming here to get the candidates to open up a bit about their work process. For example, you might zero in on a fairly complex section in one of their samples and ask how they got and processed the information in it. Did they reach out to the SMEs, read the specs, read the code, test the software themselves, report bugs, create their own mockups when the software wasn't ready before their deadline, etc.?

5. Work ethic – while the assumed or actual work contract between companies and employees may have changed significantly in recent years, and while you as a manager cannot expect (nor should you!) that your employees live only to work and await your phone calls on weekends asking them to come into the office, you still want to know if candidates have a good work ethic. Do they care about their work, or are they merely punching a clock? Ask them about deadline crunches and how they handle them. And, aside from the hiring process, make sure that you reward your team when they put in extra effort to meet deadlines with quality products. That's part of the work ethic for good managers!

Multitasking

In some organizations, this may not be relevant. In others, it's crucial. Sometimes your trainers need to juggle multiple projects, prioritize them correctly, and bring them in on time and on quality as best as possible using the decision-making criteria that apply in your specific situation.

For example, your trainers may work both on customer training and internal training for your company. When deadlines collide, your policy may be to give priority to customer training. But priority does not always mean ignoring all else, and this is where multitasking comes in.

You may want to ask candidates about the kinds of work conditions they're comfortable in, with regard here to balancing competing needs of different projects with at least partially overlapping schedules. If multitasking ability is important to you, it will help you to know whether a candidate can handle some juggling or needs the serene focus of a single assignment in order to produce.

Productivity

There are at least three aspects of productivity that you can try to assess; there may be others applicable to your organization, too.

1. Prioritizes tasks – how acute is the trainer's vision in terms of recognizing which tasks are more important or urgent? Of course, the two are not the same – important tasks can be long-term ones, and urgent tasks can, regretfully, sometimes be unimportant. But given the calculus of your group's priorities, does the trainer show – in samples, in the interview, in the test, in references – an understanding of how to prioritize conflicting tasks?

2. Meets deadlines – this is the next step in the productivity department. It's one thing to have the tasks properly prioritized. It's another to get them done, at least with the quality that is achievable given the time and other resources available for each. If deadlines are deadlines in your company or organization, look for a trainer who understands this and gets the

work done on time – again, given the constraints of time and other resources, at the highest possible quality.

3. Fast learner – part of the measure of a trainer's productivity is how much time you and others need to spend on the trainer's training. You will want to assess whether the trainer is a quick learner, who not only grasps things quickly but runs with them and soon knows more than you do on the subject. Good trainers are not regurgitators of information spoon-fed to them by subject matter experts; they need to acquire near-expert level knowledge of the subject so they can write intelligently about it in the lessons and deliver the class. You can get a sense of how fast a learner a trainer may be by asking questions about the timing for the project whose samples the trainer brings to show you.

4. Attention to detail – this shouldn't be an issue for most trainers. Attention to detail is simply part of the job. But when you are evaluating candidates, you need to be cognizant of the fact that not all candidates may have this quality. True, in some cases, a big-picture trainer can work well with a detail-oriented editor to produce quality work. But more often, you won't be able to afford the luxury of a trainer who doesn't get down to details. You want someone who sees and understands and can

train the details, just as you want someone who gets the big picture, too.

5. References – ah, such a sticky issue. HR departments in many companies, whether under orders from the legal department or just in fear of a lawsuit, will forbid former managers from discussing an employee. At all. You will get transferred to HR, who will only tell you name, rank, and serial number. That is, they will only confirm the dates of employment for the individual in question, and that's about it. So your task is to get real references. Call up the references that the candidate has listed, and ask them if they would hire the person again. Tell them an attribute or two that you are looking for in a candidate, and ask if they would feel comfortable in your choice were you to choose the trainer in question. Better yet, network with other managers, whether in ASTD (American Society for Training & Development) or other training networks, so you can ask these questions informally after a society meeting, for example. Also, use your online network, and check the candidate's online profile and references as well.

With these or other criteria defined, so you know what you're looking for, you can work with HR to create a "job req" – that is, a job requisition. Whether your recruiter uses this write-up to search online for candidates or create an ad in the paper or online, it will now reflect your considered judgement of what your company actually needs. Without this, job reqs tend to focus overly much on tools, because recruiters have to have *some* criteria by which to search; if you don't give them what you really need, they'll fall back on the externals of what software and version you use to create training materials, and that would be missing the point in a big way.

Evaluate the resumes

You might not be a trainer yourself, but you can read! Look at the resumes – and the cover letters. Are they really well-written? Do they tell you this person's story in an interesting way? Are they error-free? Next, do you see the progression or level of experience that you expect? Is this person close enough to your requirements list to move on to the next step?

Some trainers use the t-letter format as the heart of the cover letter, which presents a direct comparison of your job req's specs and the candidate's experience. It shows, presumably, that the trainer can identify and organize critical information, which I think is crucial in a training candidate. You might look for strong introductory and concluding paragraphs with some sharp writing with additional information about the candidate and why they might be great for the company and position, in addition to the direct comparison of the t-letter. The trainer should have thrown in some nice formatting for good measure.

In other words, you want to see both good writing and good organization of information, with attention to visual presentation. And in an age where basic information on your company is readily available on the net, at least the cover letter ought to reflect a little research into what your company does.

Compare the resumes with your list or spreadsheet of requirements, and invite the most promising matches in for interviews. If you have quantified the requirements in a spreadsheet, you probably have a stronger case for the fairness of your hiring decisions each step of the way, as long as your criteria are valid, because it will be plain to see why you invited in some candidates (the ones with higher scores) and not others (the ones with lower scores). You can, and should, assign weights to the criteria based on their relative importance to your company. For trainers, accuracy, aptitude, and communications skills rank up there among the highest; experience with the particular tools you use might rank lower, because you can usually teach a good trainer new tools.

This is not to suggest that hiring is an exact science and can be reduced to numbers on a spreadsheet. It's not; it's also very much an art, because it involves human beings, and humans are not entirely quantifiable. Your job is to do your best to define what you actually need in a trainer, and then be as rigorous as you can in finding the best possible matches. Anything less would be ignoring your fiduciary duty to your company. And bad matches in hiring serve no one.

Interview the trainers

Interview techniques for trainers are probably not much different than for others. Basically, the interview is an opportunity for both sides to get to know each other a bit to see if there's a possible match. Just like when interviewing for other positions, you should ask open-ended, experiential questions about the candidate's past work projects listed on the resume.

If you ask candidates whether they get along with others, they'll all say yes. But you can get more useful information if you ask them to explain the details of how they got and processed the information for the project that they did last year. Look for details on who they worked with, and how.

Start with conversation openers, then move on to general, open-ended questions, and then drill down to get the specifics you want, based in part on answers that pique your curiosity.

Questions to ask about a candidate's education

When I was a hiring manager, what people had studied in college was of very little significance to me. Probably more English majors came for interviews than others, but there were plenty of others, too.

What I was interested in was how they went about learning. Some of the best interview discussions were (in part) about art history or French or physics or whatever, subjects that interested the candidates. I learned a lot about them by asking what interested them in their subject of choice, and by asking them to tell me how they had journeyed from that subject to training.

I was looking for people who were naturally inquisitive, people with a natural ability and desire to transmit knowledge to others. And one way to begin to see this is to find out what they like to learn and why it interests them.

Questions to ask about a candidate's resume

If for some incredibly compelling reason you have chosen to invite someone in for an interview whose resume had errors in it, perhaps if their experience is so amazingly relevant to the job that you have granted a mental stay of execution, by all means ask about the problem in the resume. That's a worthwhile question whether the error was grammatical or logical. "I see here that you put the period after the closing quotation mark. Do you prefer the British usage on that, does this reflect your time as a programmer, or do you think it's clearer this way? Or (smile here), was it just a typo?"

The answer you get can be revealing. If the candidate brushes off the question as irrelevant, that's not a very good sign. But if the answer is, for example, that she does this because her technical audiences prefer it, and proceeds to briefly share an anecdote where she learned to meet this particular learner audience expectation, that can actually be a plus and not a minus.

Other resume questions might include why the candidate chose a nonstandard format, which can launch a usability conversation, or details about who the candidate worked with at a previous job ("Were you there when they were doing the Galaxy project?"), and of course details about the projects the candidate worked on.

This is not something to treat lightly. You want the candidate to be able to describe in detail what exactly they did for a given project. Ask them about how they went about getting the information. Ask about the challenges they faced and how they got past them. Ask about their co-workers. Ask about their relationships with their SMEs. Ask about what they did to get the information they needed when it was not readily available. Ask which project they liked the best, and probe the reasons why. Ask which project they liked the least, and find out why.

These questions are intended to help you find out something about the candidate's work style. Of course, it's natural for candidates to try to put their past work in a favorable light, and that's not a crime.

Your job as interviewer is to get them talking in detail about their past work, ideally with only brief questions from you to refocus their narrative when necessary. It's your best way to try to figure out whether their work characteristics will be a good match with the ones you need from them. And it's also a good way to weed out charlatans who make big claims on their resumes but can't describe what they did on those impressive projects in satisfactory detail.

Remember, keep the questions open-ended ("Tell me about a time when..." or "I see you wrote a manual for Acme on their electronic backscratcher; how does that work?"). Then, as they answer, pay attention to what they say and how comfortable they appear in recalling the details.

Drill down with questions on details where appropriate ("How did you get the information you needed from your SME in the Antarctica data center?" or "How do you program the electronic backscratcher for left-handed users?"). Your purpose here is not to conduct industrial espionage, especially if the candidate currently works for a competitor of yours. Your purpose is to probe with questions the answers to which will show whether the trainer knows what he or she is talking about – and presumably wrote about – and whether the trainer can be a part of your team.

Review the samples

Some hiring managers put great stock in the samples that candidates bring in, but others don't, for two reasons: first, they're not hard to fake, and second, it can be hard to evaluate quality without understanding the context in which the samples were produced, especially if they were from an industry unfamiliar to you. If you have a team of trainers that the candidate would be joining, have them go over the samples while you interview, and then have them join in for detailed questions on the samples.

The typical procedure, especially for a candidate who has been contracting, is to bring a portfolio with samples in it. Normally, they will have a few preselected from their repertoire. The pros will also have other samples ready to go based on the questions you ask in the interview. If you ask about their experience training CRM systems, out come the materials for those classes. If you ask about the Moon Exploration project they worked on, out comes the *Student Workbook: Lunar Rover Propulsion Systems.*

When you look at samples, ask the kinds of open-ended questions described in the previous section, and then drill down where a question occurs to you. During an interview, you don't have time to review the samples in detail. And some may contain proprietary information – which actually means that the trainer is not allowed to even show them to you, but which in my experience has meant that they will show them to you briefly but not let them out of their direct control. In other words, you can look, but not make copies to read later.

There are two, or perhaps three, reasons to look at the samples. One is to see if there are any glaring problems with them. That is, if this is what the trainer is bringing you to show off, and it's ugly or has errors, there's a problem. (Incidentally, this is not universally the case: it's possible that the trainer pulls out an imperfect sample as part of an answer to your question about whether they've ever worked on a project with an immutable deadline that just wasn't realistic. A workbook that has a few placeholders where screenshots weren't available is, in this particular case, not a bad thing. On the contrary, it means the trainer was able to swallow his or her pride in order to help the company achieve the business objective of delivering the class on time even in difficult circumstances.)

The second reason to look at the samples is to see how the candidate presents information. Not the samples themselves, but the portfolio, that is. In other words, if you look at the portfolio of samples as a collective document, how does the trainer organize, package, and present the information in it? This will give you an indication of how they organize information for training classes, too.

The third reason is to actually analyze the samples themselves, and (if time allows) to grade them on as objective a scale as you can create. The precise criteria to evaluate samples will vary from company to company, but you will certainly want to judge what the candidates present as their best work for its accuracy, clarity, creativity, instructional design principles, freedom from errors, readability, logical flow, and completeness.

Yes, without knowing all the details of the product being trained in the sample, you can't always know 100% whether the sample is accurate or not. But after you have looked at enough training packages, and especially after you have created or managed the creation of enough training packages, you will be able to tell a good one from a bad one. You will be able to tell when options are left uncovered or when steps are left out. You will be able to tell when a workbook is designed thoughtfully and anticipates a learner's thought process.

One way to benefit from multiple perspectives (and to empower your team) is to have team members review samples from candidates while you are interviewing or testing the candidate. It can be very helpful for your existing team to feel that they have a voice in the hiring process. After all, they're the ones who will likely be working closely with the person you hire. For all concerned, it's important that they be able to work well with each other.

Give a test

I had been working for a time as an independent translator and editor. This went fine for quite some time until a major client stopped paying its bills due to internal budget problems. Very quickly, I decided that the joys of independence had to be replaced with a steadier income. I got my first job as a technical writer and trainer in the mid-1980s, when software development was becoming quite a big business, by simply answering an ad.

Well, it wasn't really that simple. The company sent all candidates to a series of detailed intelligence and other tests, which my boss later told me he did not particularly believe in. What he did trust as a test is amazingly simple. In this company, tech writers had two primary tasks: editing documents, and writing new ones based on information from a programmer.

So the test had two parts. In part one, the boss gave me a particularly badly written real document fragment, and asked me to edit it. In part two, the boss sat down, took on the *persona* of a programmer, and explained a complicated algorithm to me in programmers' language. It was my task to produce a document based on this conversation, just as writers do in reality.

Some time after I began working for the company, my boss revealed the Secret of the Test. It seems most people want to add their own brilliant angle to what the programmer tells them, or leave key information out, or reorganize the information so as to make it unintelligible. To pass the test, candidates had to do only this: intelligently interpret what the programmer said, capture all the important information, and write it in a readable document. Why? Because that's what tech writers did in their everyday work there at that time. (Only later did we begin doing technical training.)

The purpose of a test

Some people (and HR departments) object passionately to this, but it seems abundantly clear that the best way to see whether candidates are able to perform a job is to give a test that approximates what they would be doing on the job. Don't demean trainer candidates with simplistic tests if they do not replicate what your company produces.

It's far more useful to have them produce an hour's worth of work on something that resembles what you actually do. If the job involves taking a convoluted specification and extracting the relevant information from it in order to make a first draft of a training lesson, take an old spec and have them work on it. You can simplify or shorten the test to keep it in a reasonable time frame for the candidate. Give detailed instructions, and see if they follow them.

You will be amazed at how some candidates who might seem unpromising in the interview show that they can really produce in the test. And vice versa. Of all the criteria, the test is probably the single best predictor of success on the job – provided that you construct a good test!

Designing a good test

So, what constitutes a good test? A test for employment should be *valid, reliable,* and *nondiscriminatory*. A *valid* test does what it sets out to do: it accurately measures candidates' ability to do what you are trying to test. If you need a trainer, one who understands the deepest intricacies of helicopter engines or the sales process or whatever, a spelling and grammar test won't tell you if a candidate has this quality or not. It would not be a valid test.

To be *reliable*, a test has to produce consistent results over time. If you construct a test that the same person will achieve a similar result on each time, that's one indication of reliability. Another is that different people will grade the same test similarly.

So, for example, if you have designed a valid test that measures candidates' aptitude and knowledge of the sales process, and part of the test is to design a lesson on overcoming common objections to your company's product or something similar, the test can be said to be reliable if multiple reviewers grade each candidate's output in a similar way. In other words, if one reviewer gives a candidate a B+ and another gives a D, that's not a good indication of reliability in the test.

To sum up so far: *validity* means that you're testing the right material. *Reliability* means that your test produces consistent results; you give the same test to all candidates, and the scores can be measured consistently. (Not that all candidates will score the same!)

Finally, a test must be nondiscriminatory. You must not create a test that discriminates against any legally protected group. For example, there is no reason to use example names in your test that might be identifiable as belonging to a particular ethnic group. But nondiscrimination extends far beyond the text you use in a test; especially in the United States, you must be aware of legal requirements and guidelines in order to avoid getting yourself and your company in serious legal trouble. A simple briefing with your HR department is likely all you need to learn how to avoid discriminatory practices in hiring and employment.

When to test

Give the test to candidates who successfully get through the interview with samples. Try to design it to reflect the skills you're really looking for. The single best way to see how well someone would do is to simulate, as closely as possible, what you'd want them to do on the job. I also think this is a good way to help neutralize any personal biases, because it's an attempt to measure performance, not personality.

Sometimes interviewees who seem nice and all that just can't put together the simulated lesson – they don't address the stated needs of the users, or they leave out critical information, or they just don't have a clue how to create a training lesson. The last thing you want is to hire them and *then* have to deal with the problems that will surely result.

It's not realistic, nor is it fair, to ask candidates to come out for a full day and do real work for you, even though that might be a better approximation of what you want to measure. Nor is it less than insulting to ask trainers to write a lesson on how to make a sandwich, unless you work for a restaurant chain and will need to create training programs for the chain's kitchen staff. What you want to do is to come up with a test that realistically captures the key items you're seeking.

A sample test

Here is a sample test I've used that is intended to measure a candidate's ability to produce a short training lesson.

> *A spaceship lands in the parking lot, and its Martian passengers are eager to make contact with the White House. Our guests understand simple English, and have heard that there is a communications device called the telephone that they might use to accomplish this task.*
>
> *Please create a short lesson for our guests from Mars so they can complete their mission.*

It uses a common device – the telephone – with which any candidate will be quite familiar. It introduces aliens from another planet (clearly not part of any Earthly ethnic group), who have not used a telephone before, so that the trainers will be challenged to explain how to use the phone without skipping steps or assuming knowledge that isn't there. It quietly calls attention to the need for simple language on the part of the trainer by indicating that the Martians understand simple (but not complicated) English. And it also tells the attentive trainer to focus on the "mission" at hand – making one phone call successfully – instead of writing a treatise on the principles of telephony.

For an organization whose trainers need to create training lessons – training the step-by-step procedures of tasks in simple language – the test is a valid one. It measures just that.

When I gave this test, I chose not to define a time limit for the candidates. While it's true that better reliability might be achieved if each candidate were given precisely the same amount of time, my managerial instinct said that candidates are naturally nervous, and while I might take into account how long they worked on their test in relation to the quality they produced, nothing much would be achieved by adding to their nervousness with an arbitrary deadline enforced with a stopwatch. In other words, I opted to increase the validity of the test at, perhaps, a small cost in reliability. Most people spent about the same time on the test, with only a few outliers being much shorter or longer.

Some trainers went to town with this test, showing professionalism, good training design, and humor. Some included placeholders for graphics, some imagined including Martian equivalents for English terms. Perhaps surprisingly, but not to me, not all trainers did well on the test – even those whose resumes or samples looked good. Those who did well on the test, and who were eventually hired, did very well on the job. Those who did not – well, we thanked them for their time.

A good test really serves its purpose and takes a lot of guesswork and emotional hunches out of the hiring process. It may also save you legal heartache if someone threatens a suit based on a hiring decision; you can point to the test and say, with good reason, that your decision was results-based. Keep the test results of all candidates in your files, along with their resumes and your notes.

Chapter 8
Managing a training group in a corporate environment

The role of trainers in a corporate environment

As a training manager, one of your most important roles is to manage everyone's expectations in a healthy way, both inside and outside your group. If you can do this successfully and on an ongoing basis, you will make an enormous contribution to the morale of your trainers and of the people who work with them, and this will help make sure that the training goes out on time with the right content.

How do you do this?

Educate your trainers

First, within your group: educate your trainers about their role in your corporate environment. Chances are, the training group is not the model ship around which the glass bottle of the rest of the company was blown. For many companies, training is a cost center, and is seen as a necessary evil. Engineers have an understandable tendency to see trainers as pests, because they always want to create the training program at the same time that the engineers are busy creating, testing, and debugging the product.

If this is the case for your company, you need to work with your trainers to keep your group as efficient as possible, not only to reduce costs, but in particular to reduce the time costs of your trainers in producing what they need to produce.

So make sure that your training actually adds value. Train your trainers to work with the product and with the SMEs to create excellent, or at least very good, training courses. The result will be that your trainers will know that they are adding to the value of the product.

And the secondary result will be that the people they work with directly – the subject matter experts, primarily – will recognize this, too.

Educate your company

Second, in the larger context of the company, you owe it to yourself and your trainers to subtly advocate for the value in your training. It's not necessary, and in fact it would likely be counterproductive, to send out emails or announce meetings with the subject being the glorious contributions of your group.

But when you meet individually with other managers, or in larger meetings, you can and should show, when appropriate, that your group manages to the same kinds of metrics that everyone else does, and that it approaches its tasks with the same seriousness and vision of the company's larger needs as any other group.

So, imagine a meeting about a new product. Get yourself invited, if you aren't already, by telling the meeting organizer that you want to be there from the start to make sure that you understand what the training needs and challenges will be. In the meeting, ask intelligent questions about the product and its target users, its antecedents in earlier products, project timelines, and all the rest. Come prepared with your own metrics, so that you can give ballpark estimates of the required training effort: "Let's see…you're estimating 20 new screens…using our averages, that should mean a training effort on the order of 2.4 person-months, depending on some specific variables that we'll evaluate later on in the project, so that we can fine-tune our estimates using the stats we collect from all our projects."

The minute you start talking the language of the other project managers – estimates, person-months, project tracking, and contingency planning – you will show that your group consists of professionals whose work is done using some of the same tools and methodologies as everybody else on the development team.

How to be professional when others aren't

Sometimes all your concerted efforts to establish a professional tone in your relations with colleagues in the company will not help. When this happens, remember to focus on what you actually need to do to serve the company and its customers.

The weirdest thing I ever had to do as a manager was to go shopping for sheets (yes, the kind you sleep on). We had a customer coming in for software training, and the classrooms weren't available. So I booked a conference room. It was a small class, and that was a sensible alternative. A VP in charge of nothing in particular heard that I was going to put computers on the beautiful soft-wood table he had picked out so lovingly, and wanted me to cancel the course. I won, since it was for a customer, and the course was not cancelled. But the VP insisted that I get a table covering, so his beautiful table would not be marred by customer-induced scratches.

It was the day before the class, and there was no way I could get a custom-fit table pad in time for the long, oval conference table. So I went shopping for the thickest tablecloth I could find. All the cloths were floral or other patterns and colors not appropriate for an office setting. So I got solid-color sheets instead, folded them over a few times, and taped them down onto the table. The course could proceed.

I bet it was the only time the company ever purchased bed sheets. Well, I hope so, anyway.

In this case, I suppose I could have made a fuss with the VP's boss, the division president. But the professional thing to do, it seemed to me then and now, was to make sure that the training course went on as scheduled with minimum disruption. The fact that the VP had nothing better to do than try to protect his ill-considered selection of a soft wood for the conference table was annoying, but irrelevant to me.

So be prepared, when necessary, to be unconventional and adaptive instead of rigid, because sometimes this is how you can best maintain professionalism in the work that you and your group do.

The training team

Except in very small companies, there is usually a team of trainers and others that are collectively responsible for the company's training. You may be a manager of precisely one trainer, namely yourself, but chances are that you manage at least a small team.

If your team is small, it likely consists of a few trainers, with little or no distinction in their respective job roles. When I built small teams of trainers and writers, this was the pattern. Dedicated editor or artist positions come in larger teams; small teams have to fend for themselves in these areas.

That means that you have to be especially mindful in the hiring process if your team is a small one where, typically, trainers edit each other's work because there is no dedicated editor. Or, depending on your other responsibilities, the editor might be you, at least in the beginning. The mindfulness in building a team is necessary to ensure that you hire people who are willing to work together, who follow a defined if flexible set of standards, and who respect each other's work. If they have some complementary skill sets, so much the better.

One of your most defining tasks as a manager – because it will define the success of your team – is to build a solid team. Since you will be hiring adults, you can skip the fake team-building exercises that seem so common in corporate training programs. What they accomplish is the building of fake teams, or perhaps the fake building of teams. You, on the other hand, need to build a real team.

So how do you do this? First and foremost, by example. If you are busy posturing as The Boss instead of leading and guiding, you are making a very unproductive mistake. You should be able to not only describe the essence of the work you need your team to do, but also be able to codify how to get that work done.

I do not mean that you should write an Employee Manual. That's for HR to write, and a copy belongs in every desk drawer, right underneath the boxes of extra staples and paper clips. But you should definitely write at least the initial version of your team's Standards document (see the next section), in which you define what goes in each kind of document your team produces and how it gets there. As your team matures, your team members can take over this document.

Define standards

The purpose of a Standards document is to set out clearly what you expect your trainers to produce and how they are to do it. The structure of your Standards should be built around the kinds of deliverables that you produce, with a chapter devoted to each.

So, for example, let's assume that your team creates student workbooks, instructor guides, online learning, performance support, and other training products for your customers. Chapters with those names will appear in your Standards document. Within each chapter, explain what the deliverable is and how to create it.

Continuing the example, your document outline might look like this:

Chapter 1 – Introduction and Scope

Chapter 2 – Creating Student Workbooks

Chapter 3 – Creating Instructor Guides

Chapter 4 – Creating Online Learning

Chapter 5 – Creating Performance Support

Fleshing out the outline a little more might result in something like this:

[...]

Chapter 2 – Creating Student Workbooks

2.1 – How to Structure a Student Workbook Using Task-Based Lessons

2.2 – Dealing with Format Issues

2.3 – Dealing with Style Issues

[...]

And this outline, in turn, might be fleshed out like this:

[...]

Chapter 2 – Creating Student Workbooks

2.1 – How to Structure a Student Workbook Using Task-Based Lessons

2.1.1 – Writing the Lesson Objective

2.1.2 – Writing the Lesson Overview

2.1.3 – Writing the Task Procedure

2.1.4 – Writing the Task Example

2.1.5 – Writing the Task Review

2.2 – Dealing with Format Issues

2.3 – Dealing with Style Issues

[...]

Within each of these sections, to continue with the example, tell your trainers directly what kind of information to put in. Use examples, so there is no doubt about what you expect.

The resulting chapter might look something like this:

[...]

Chapter 2 – Creating Student Workbooks

Student workbooks are not user guides, and do not document every feature of the system. Indeed, they are not even organized around system functions, but instead around user tasks, going from simple to complex and from common to rare. Student workbooks contain everything learners need – but nothing more – in order to do the most common and important tasks in their jobs using the new system. Tasks are not equal to system functions. Tasks are activities that humans perform in order to achieve some objective.

In our company, tasks are things that users in a customer organization do as part of their jobs. The student workbook must therefore give these users what they need in order to get started using the system. Unlike our user guides, which cover every task that involves the system, training materials cover only common tasks. There are two reasons for this:

In training, new users don't learn about every glorious feature of the system. They just learn what they need to be able to do their jobs – that is, to perform common tasks using the system.

But sometimes, on the job, users need to perform complex tasks or tasks that are not common. Since it would be counterproductive to try to teach every single task in training – the unfortunate students would only forget most of the material – they are taught in our training programs to refer to the user guide as a complete task-based reference.

Therefore, our user guides are comprehensive, and our customers expect them to include every system-oriented task. Our training materials are focused, by comparison, on the essentials.

2.1 – How to Structure a Student Workbook Using Tasks

Based on your study of each of the job roles for users of your system, build a list of tasks. Organize the tasks into logical groups, and put the groups in chronological order of performance, where there is such an order, and otherwise from simple to complex and from common to rare. If there are dependencies between groups, put the prerequisite tasks before the dependent ones.

This ordered list of tasks is the outline of your student workbook. The logical groups are the lessons, and the tasks within each group are the first-level sections.

For each task, include the following sub-sections:

- Task Objective
- Task Overview
- Task Procedure
- Task Example
- Task Review

These are described below.

2.1.1 – Writing the Task Objective

Every task must have an objective: what will the reader do in this task? Write the objective in terms of the business or system tasks they will do. It can be a single sentence or even a bullet list. For example:

In this task, you will do the following:

- Start MCS
- Search for a customer by various search criteria
- Locate information about the customer in the customer folder

This lets users know what they are about to do. This is good: it helps reduce any anxiety, and it helps focus the users on the task. It also lets them verify that this is the task they need.

2.1.2 – Writing the Task Overview

Here is where you introduce the task and any major concepts involved. Don't go into details or procedure steps here; that is for the heart of the task section.

This conceptual material is important for complex tasks, because it explains the business situations in which the task is performed.

Not all tasks require introduction of new concepts. If you are writing how to change passwords, for example, you can keep the overview short, because most users are quite familiar with the concept of passwords. If, however, you are explaining the method that the new system uses to organize customer information, then it is important to cover this concept so that you can then proceed with the actual steps.

2.1.3 – Writing the Task Procedure

Walk the user through the task in a step-by-step procedure. Make each step a third-level subsection. Since this is a student workbook, include appropriate screen captures with callouts and cutouts to illustrate as needed. (We do not include screen captures in online help, because the screen is already visible.)

[...]

2.1.4 – Writing the Task Example

Include only the main steps from the procedure; omit the substeps, though you can refer to them if necessary for clarity. Include screen captures at half-size.

[...]

2.1.5 – Writing the Task Review

Summarize the main steps as follows:

To [name of the task]:

[task procedure step one]

[task procedure step two]

[...]

[task procedure step *n*]

2.2 – Dealing with Format Issues

Include only command key options in the procedure. Put the icons for buttons as alternatives in the left margin, using the standard template.

[...]

2.3 – Dealing with Style Issues

As in all of our training materials and documentation, use active voice. Speak to the reader in your own words instead of reciting to a faceless entity.

[...]

The purpose of your Standards document, as seen in these outline and content snippets, is to detail for your trainers just what you need them to produce and how to produce it. With your Standards document in hand, a new trainer or a trainer charged with doing a new task can actually get to work.

Standards are important, because you will want your group's documents to include similar kinds of information across multiple products. Why? So that the documents will be easier for your group to maintain going forward, so that one trainer can without difficulty serve as instructor for a course that another trainer wrote (think of pilots who use standard procedures to do similar work in different planes), and so that your readers can easily navigate through your documents to find what they need using a standard approach.

There are definitely times when you will choose to ignore a part of one of your standards, perhaps due to a different kind of product being trained, or perhaps due to customization of your training for a particular customer who either needs or prefers a different setup. Standards, after all, are standards – which means in most industries and organizations that they should usually be followed – but they are not usually life-and-death requirements. When you need to adapt them, you should. After all, that's your job as a manager.

Distribute the work in your team

One of the more challenging parts of your job as a manager is finding an optimal distribution of assignments to your team members. (Obviously, if your team consists of just you, that's not a distribution problem, but instead a time management and priorities issue.) Once you have even one other member of your group, you need to decide how to break up and distribute the work.

It helps enormously if you have been able to select team members based in part on their team skills (or if you have been enormously fortunate and have inherited such a team). Some team members may not play well together, and it is possible that you will want them on your team nonetheless if they are just that good at their work on their own, even though this will present challenges to you and their colleagues over time.

How structured you need to be in your group depends largely on the size of the group. If you have three or four trainers, you probably do not have and cannot afford a dedicated editor, graphic artist, or performance support system technologist. So your trainers will be on their own – in their instructional design, that is. You have two options for editing and quality control in this setup: yourself, or peer editing.

The manager as editor

This option works well when you know the material well and you know the standards, both written and unwritten, that you want the training materials to adhere to. For small teams, it often makes great sense for the manager to serve as the group editor.

When you are the editor, you are of necessity involved hands-on in the work of your team. You will know exactly what they are producing, because you will be editing it. This is your chance – and your obligation – to help your trainers catch their omissions, their slips in logic, their assumptions of learner knowledge that might be unfounded, their redundancies, and yes, their writing errors, if any. Just by sending back a version of their file marked richly (but not unnecessarily) with helpful comments from you, you can help your trainers grow professionally.

Peer editing

The other option for small teams is for trainers to review each other's work. It's possible that these reviews might not turn up every gem that you would find, but this is the way to go if you do not have the time to do the editing. Peer editing depends, naturally, much more on goodwill among the trainers. You have to establish standards for editing and the tone that will work for your people. In some organizations, sensitivities run high, and peer editors will need to note this when they write up their comments. In other organizations, more direct communication is okay.

Dedicated editors

If your group is large enough, hire a dedicated editor, or contract with one for as-needed work. This person will be responsible for editing the output of the trainers, and need not be a trainer (although it is also possible to have a part-time editor whose other duties include instructional design as well). If you are hiring a dedicated editor, you can look for more editing skills and experience than you might require of a trainer who will be asked to peer-edit the work of other trainers. Give a detailed editing test that includes the usual sorts of grammar and syntax mistakes, but be sure that it also includes tests for the ability to edit for logic, meaning, completeness, redundancy, adherence to standards, and accuracy – and, above all, good instructional design.

Involve the trainers

There are managers whose approach seems to be to let underlings know only what they need to in order to perform a task. But assembly lines have given up this philosophy, and it certainly is counterproductive in a training team. Yes, you don't always have time for theoretical discussions about process improvements when there is a deliverable to get out the door, and you also don't want to constantly revisit decisions about the team standards. But as a general rule, it is both good and necessary to involve your team members in the bigger picture of your team's work.

What might this include?

Maintain a whiteboard with current and near-term future projects and assignments listed for all to see.

Have regular weekly meetings with the purpose not of having each team member sit through everyone else's status report – that level of detail is best managed directly between you and each trainer – but instead with the purpose of communicating with the team about what's going on in the company, what projects are in the pipeline for the team, general team issues, etc.

Keep your door open, not closed, except when truly necessary. What you are working on should rarely be a secret to your team, and an open door will encourage team members to drop in on you – just as you should be dropping in on them. Informal communication on an ongoing basis almost always beats formal meetings in terms of efficient use of both people's time, not to mention good working relations, unless your team is very large.

Bring team members to meetings with other teams when relevant and when time allows, so that not all information has to flow only through you. You will actually grow as a leader when your team members grow, and giving them exposure to the bigger picture of your organization will help them, you, and the company.

When project time, importance, and risk allow, encourage your trainers to learn new items in your company's product line, new technologies, new techniques and tools, and whatever else you can think of to keep things interesting for them and to allow them to grow in value to your team and company.

When it's time to estimate a new project, involve your trainers in the work of estimating the number and size (small, medium, large) of tasks to be trained, and discuss the results with them as you apply their estimates to your estimation spreadsheet.

When you are interviewing for a new hire, involve the members of your team in the interview and testing process. If two heads are better than one, multiple gut feelings – and yes, my gut joins me in speaking from experience – are better still. One or more of your team members may pick up on something that you miss entirely.

Build teams

What can you do to build your team, aside from hiring good or great people to begin with?

The most important thing you can do is to set a tone of cooperation, respect, and friendship through personal example. Involving your trainers in more than the direct details of their tasks, as described in the previous section, is an extraordinarily important first step in showing them how they should relate to each other, to others in the company, and of course to you, because you will have demonstrated this yourself.

You can also have two or more trainers work together on large projects, or on separate pieces of projects, so that they learn to trust each other's abilities and work output. You can encourage a team atmosphere at work without resorting to the silliness that seems to plague some offices by making needed space for humor, shared goodies at team meetings, celebration of personal and professional milestones, and showing your team members that you do care about them as people, not only as employees.

If and as your group grows, promote from within. There is little more demoralizing to a dedicated team member who has worked hard on your projects than to have a new supervisor drop in seemingly by parachute to be their new boss. It not only says that your original team members aren't good enough, but it also says that anyone can come in and successfully manage them without the detailed knowledge that the trainers have built up over the years. If you don't want your trainers to feel like lions being tamed, help them grow professionally and promote from within when you have the opportunity to do so. Of course, there may be specific skills that you need in a new hire, and these skills might not reside in one of your current employees. For example, say your team's growth now allows you to have a technologist on staff; your instructional designers and trainers might not have that set of IT skills, and so you will by necessity need to look outside your organization.

Once you have a structure of trainers reporting to team leaders reporting to you, or with multiple layers if your department grows to be exceptionally large – and note that it's really only possible for anyone to directly supervise three to five people effectively, so that if you have more than that number of teams, you will need more layers of management – you will do well to balance your need for direct knowledge of what is going on in each project with the need to delegate and to show your trust in the teams' ability to do their work and report to you on their progress and the issues or obstacles they face.

Monitor the work and communications

With one or two trainers reporting directly to you in a small training group, this is easy: you simply look over the cubicle wall to find out what's going on. When you have thirty trainers reporting ultimately to you through team leaders and project leaders, monitoring your group's work and communications becomes that much more challenging – yet no less important.

So how do you keep informed of what's going on? In some organizations – unfortunately, perhaps many – everyone has to fill out detailed status reports every week. An hour a week, 2.5% of the valuable work time of each and every employee, is spent filling out a formal document where they have to report arbitrary percentages of task completion, issues, goals for next week, and so on. That's really overkill. In organizations that track time for billing purposes, special time codes are created for the purpose of filling in these lengthy reports. And pity the poor manager who has to at least pretend to read them all with sufficient attention, along with all of the manager's other duties. And as a manager, think about it: do you really want to add 2.5% to your team's overhead, time that they could otherwise be spending more productively?

It seems to me that there are really only two ways to intelligently monitor a group's work, including both progress and issues/obstacles, so that you know what's going on and can react in near-real time to roadblocks that come up. The first is to use hard data: the project plan for each project should be managed constantly and meticulously, with each project leader updating the tasks that get completed. Any task that falls behind schedule will become immediately apparent. Upstream managers – again, ultimately that would be you – can and must see these slippages in the project plan without waiting for a wordy report. You should have the project plan constantly open on your screen for most or all of your current projects, or at least check them daily.

The second method, which is used in tandem with the first, is constant, ongoing, organic communication back and forth, focusing on areas in the project plan that you've already identified as carrying the greatest risk (both in terms of likelihood of a problem and of severity of a problem if it does in fact come to pass) and on any areas that you see are beginning to fall behind. Walk over to the team leader or member responsible for the task and ask what's up.

If a subject matter expert has not been available, you can work with the SME or the SME's manager to get the SME's time freed up. (Or, if you can't, you can at least document the issue and escalate to *your* manager; the resolution may in some cases be that you have to be patient, but you need to cover your rear about the delay and the impact it will have on what your team can produce.)

If there's some other issue, the only way to find out is to ask. Some give-and-take in a project plan as the ideal of estimates hits the world of reality is normal; some tasks will take a bit longer than expected, and some shorter; these should be minor and average out over the life of a project. What you need to be totally on top of is those that are taking longer. Maybe you underestimated the work. Maybe the system is not as available as expected. Maybe the trainer was out sick for two days. Maybe the trainer needs help in learning to stick to deadline. Maybe you need to assign more resources to the task, which might be something as simple as relieving the trainer of some other task responsibilities that can be pushed off or reassigned to someone else.

Don't wait for formal reports. Don't be a stranger in your own department. Get out there and let people tell you what's going on, and what isn't. There's no good reason to wait for a weekly report on a form prepared in triplicate that takes an hour to fill out.

Evaluate the trainers

Formal evaluations can be a wasteful process

In most companies, formal evaluations are done either once or twice a year. In most companies, formal evaluations suck up resources of the employees for days before the dreaded review as they try to muster up exhibits of project and personal successes to use in their defense in a process where they have little input and no control, all while the managers spend precious time filling out inordinately detailed evaluation forms that often have little to do with the actual work done in the department.

What purpose is served by this exercise in misery and drudgery?

Some organizations even go further along the path of cruelty, forcing managers to fight among each other for pieces of the bonus or raise pie for their employees. Some go so far as to insist that everyone, but *everyone*, must be ranked along a strict bell curve, with no tie rankings allowed. Each employee is defined as precisely better than one other employee and precisely worse than another.

That's not a reflection of real life. While some HR people may swear by the "objectivity" of such a system, from a business perspective, it is neither objective nor productive. It also doesn't make any sense.

Align evaluations with your hiring criteria

Yet you do need a way to evaluate your trainers and reward them for meeting and exceeding your expectations as they grow in value to your team and your company. So how might you do this fairly and economically, taking away the trauma and wasted time of the common system?

The answer is deceptively simple. You have already drawn up, and probably refined, a spreadsheet with all the criteria that you have identified as worth measuring when you evaluate candidates for hire. These criteria are based on the real world of your team's work, not some artificial set of criteria that HR pulled off a survey somewhere that has nothing to do with what your training group actually does.

Why not use this very same spreadsheet to evaluate your team members? After all, the criteria in it were scrupulously defined by you, with input from your team, from parallel teams perhaps, and from your own manager, and you have no doubt successfully defended the criteria and the relative weights of each with your HR people, so as to protect you and the company from lawsuits by people whom you did not hire. Your defense there is that the criteria are objective, valid – meaning that they actually serve as an indication of what it takes to succeed as a member of your team – and transparent – not, of course, to the candidate, but to everyone else involved in the interviewing and hiring process.

Transparent evaluations

So, that being the case, why not make use of this already-done work, and use it to evaluate your team members? There should be no surprises to them in how their work is measured: if there were, that would mean that they are flying blind, unaware of what it really is that you want out of them.

By making the criteria transparent to all, you not only gain an instant, readily measurable, evaluation tool, but you also in effect have established your team's mission statement even without putting pen to paper and framing it on the wall. As your team works on each new project that comes their way, they will already know what constitutes success in their work, and they will be able to plan their efforts accordingly without even having to ask you.

With the criteria clearly defined and known in advance, you reduce stress in the evaluation process. There are no trick questions, no secret or personal judgements being made. All it boils down to at this point is measuring each criterion for the employees and resolving any differences that may come up in your assessment and theirs. Most of the time, most people are harsher on themselves and grade themselves more critically than others see them.

If you think a team member is only average in a number of criteria, and he thinks that he is absolutely the best thing that ever happened across the board in every category, it's probably not just a difference of opinion on the criteria themselves. Chances are that, in such a case, you either need to work with the trainer to elucidate the criteria and his performance, or that you are dealing with someone who just doesn't get the simplicity of a reality-based evaluation system and still believes that he has to defend himself by going on the offensive.

Client relations

Business to consumer

If you work for a business-to-consumer company, you might include contact information in your training products for users to be able to let you know when they find a problem in the training materials after the class (and especially for online learning). You might even have a link or contact details on your company web site.

But if you are like most training groups for companies that market to consumers, you will have to work to foster any kind of relationship with your users before and after training sessions. And fostering such a relationship is important, because without contact with the people who are the customers of your training, you will be flying blind. When your management asks you to justify the existence of your training group and its associated personnel and other costs, you won't be able to point to any hard data indicating how the customers value what you do.

What you need to do to is to show why your group is needed, why you add value to the company and the product (*not* just the training product, which many managers don't value or don't know how to value, unless you charge for your training products and services!). Here is where user contact is necessary. If you can show that *users* care about the training, you can demonstrate that spending what it takes to fix or improve the training keeps customers from dumping your company's product and buying another.

This is because your training can be shown to increase user understanding and acceptance of the product. Happy users who understand how to use your product will buy new versions and spread the word about how good your product and its training are. Also, you can show that your training reduces support and possibly other costs. (If your company charges for support, the issue becomes murkier as costs partially morph into revenues; what is harder to measure is how many customers will choose not to use paid support and simply walk away from your product.)

If you can communicate directly with your users and thank them for their input – and yes, even solicit such input – you will render your company the service of giving its impersonal products a human face – yours.

Remember that in some companies, training is a cost, a necessary evil. The market demands that the product come with some kind of training, so it does. From the company's perspective, it's a cost, pure and simple, and if they could do away with it – and you – they would.

So how do you change this? By internal selling, of course.

First, here's how *not* to do it:

- Write angry (or even calm) emails about how important training is

- Write angry (or even calm) emails about how your process isn't being followed by the rest of the company and how this is just not how things should be done

- Make a presentation about the steps in your team's workflow so that everyone realizes why you need more time and budget

That said, here are some things that you *can* do:

- Manage your own budget. Even if you don't have *authority* over your budget, you can still show that you're conscious of your role in managing costs responsibly. Corporate managers will like this.

- Manage your relationship with external customers. Don't sit back and let the engineers be the exclusive conduits of information. They may get it wrong sometimes, and you know better than they what you need from the user community. Managing this customer relationship will not only improve your training, but also demonstrate that you *have* customers. That is, your company will understand that your work is actually part of the product. While you're still a cost, so are the engineers, and now you are an integral part of the core development costs, which can't be eliminated without eliminating the product altogether.

- Attend development meetings. You have to make yourself part of the overall team. Sure, it's cozy to sit off in trainerland with your buddies who understand you. But the benefits – to you and the company – of working together with the development team are enormous. You'll understand the product better, and be able to contribute, perhaps, to improvements in the product design based on your knowledge of the user community (see above). No, not every trainer can do usability and interface design. But just like it's good medicine for each of the relevant medical specialties to take part in the conference about the patient, you bring a perspective that rightly is part of the development decision-making process. Say, for example, that the programmers want to rename a button in all of the application screens. In most cases, that's a quick and easy fix for them – and a potential nightmare for you if you only find out at the last minute. Suddenly, the Compare button is gone, and there is a new button called Contrast. What does it do? If you were at the development meeting, not only would you know, but you'd be able to tell the group how long it will take you to redo the screenshots and update your references to the button, making the training part of the software change, as it should be.

Business to business

In business-to-business scenarios, it is usually much easier to establish and maintain direct contact with end users, or at least with their organizational representatives. Say you work for a software company that, instead of retail software, makes software for a particular industry. Even if the software package is a fixed one, the same for all customers, you will be able, perhaps with a little maneuvering if necessary, to make contact with your user community. Get yourself a seat at the table at design meetings. Join your company's delegation to trade shows. Volunteer to help staff the support line, whether by telephone or chat.

Learn about the industry that your company serves by keeping up on trade journals and web sites. If your company buys subscriptions, make sure you get on the distribution list; note, happily, that many trade journals are actually distributed free – all you have to do is ask the publisher for a subscription. They are happy to add you to the list, because such journals are not mass-market publications. They depend on ad revenues and on revenues from sponsoring seminars and events specific to your industry where anyone who is anyone has to fork over relatively large sums to attend. Greater circulation numbers mean the publishers can charge more for those ads.

If your company customizes its products for customers, then you are in a good place for building more direct connections with your customers. First and foremost, if the product gets customized, so must the training. You will be producing training for each customer's specific implementation, which means that you will be meeting with the developers in your company doing the customization. At a minimum, you will receive information – even if you may have to dig a bit – from the developers about the customer's specified requirements. Beyond that, you can earn a place for your team in the design meetings with the customer where those requirements are hashed out.

Serving customers directly

Once you establish direct contact with customers, you will be able to sell training products and services to them. Ideally, you will be able to establish your group as a distinct profit center in the company, where you bring in add-on revenues that otherwise would not be there.

For example, a company that sells customized products can sell – with a little help from even a one-person training department – customized training. A company that includes training with the product can create training packages for sale to customers who have training needs. That package can itself be customized (as a billable sale) for customers who want things done a particular way, or for whom the main product has been customized.

Interestingly enough, there can be times when documentation and training – which may normally be charged separately – will even be thrown in the deal by senior management to win a major account. This, of course, can only be done once these added-value products exist as sellable products/services. Either way, the value to the company is there in the numbers for all to see. You may be able to start selling add-on training products and services in your company or, almost as good and sometimes better, you may be able to help your company make more sales because of the training you can do in pre-sales meetings.

Conversely, it can be possible to sell training products and services independent of sales of your company's main offerings. This is especially so when you work in a company that "owns" an industry vertical, meaning that your company is seen as expert in the industry it serves. I once sold a project to create online help for a product that a customer was developing on their own, not one of my company's products.

While you will still manage projects at a high level (the buzzword is managing the "customer relationship"), your focus may shift into selling training projects to your company's customers. This is good for all parties, including you, because the value of your work will be just as easily demonstrable as for any employee whose efforts contribute directly to your company's revenues (what on financial statements is known as "top line") and profits (what is known on those same statements as "bottom line").

If you can transform your operations in whole or in part from a cost center to a profit center, you will be better off, and so will your company.

Offering customized training

But even if you don't get a chance to actually sell your work – say, for example, that your company throws in the customization of the training at no charge for customers paying for the software to be customized – you can still build the relationship between your team and the customer so that you add demonstrable value in assuring the customer's satisfaction with the main product.

Think of your group as friendly consultants; since the training is expressly customized for each customer, you have no reason to hide behind the product (not that there is ever a good reason to do that!). Say the software has a clunky interface that for budget or other reasons isn't going to be changed. You have the opportunity to step in and, through your training, make it possible for the customer's users to quickly adapt to the new software and help assure user acceptance and satisfaction. These are not small matters.

Serving as a bridge to the customer

In addition to helping your customer's end users, your establishment of a direct connection with the customer's training and especially business staff will allow you to serve another role, that of intermediary or bridge between the customer and its various teams, on the one hand, and your company's staff on the other. In most companies, the techies are kept very busy, and if you are able to take some of their load off their shoulders by communicating with the customer, answering level-one kinds of questions, you will be adding yet another valuable service to your company. Just make sure that you communicate regularly with your management about all the work your team does and the value it adds!

Helping customers with their own internal training

In some cases, customers prefer to create their own training, based in part on what your company provides. This is often the case where the system itself is part of a larger set of user procedures that need to be trained. Your company's training rightly focuses on the software or other product, even to the point of how users employ that product in accomplishing their work tasks. But you are not likely to be able to train non-system work procedures that are specific to the policies of your client's organization. Even if you know the industry, each client probably does business a little bit differently.

Thus, an iteration or extension of working directly with the client is that your group can sell the add-on service of helping the client create and maintain its *own* training. In other words, there is no reason why your trainers can't serve as expert consultants to your client's training team (if there is one, and often it is an *ad hoc* group only): you can cross the bridge to the client's internal training of practices, standards, etc., and thereby create a whole new service for your company to sell.

Imagine what a useful service this can be for the customer, who is usually not in the business of training new procedures to go along with the introduction of a new system. And imagine what an incredibly useful service this is for your company to be able to offer to its clients. It adds revenue, it deepens the penetration of your company and its services into the client organization, and it increases customer acceptance of and satisfaction with your company and its products.

Communicating with other groups in your organization

When you communicate with other groups – upward, downward, and horizontally across the company – figure out what the best mode of communication is with each individual or group that you need to communicate with. For some, it could well be emails or documents.

But for others, it might be a phone call, or a quick text, or an informal in-person visit to their office or cubicle, or a meeting in a conference room without interruptions, or some other medium.

If you feel the need to document such conversations, that's fine. You can send an email summarizing the main points, so that the record shows what was discussed and decided. Just don't automatically rely solely on written communication, even if you and your group naturally do it well.

Re-use, repurposing, and content management systems

Perhaps the single most distinguishing characteristic of most technical training is its disdain for originality. When you learned to write in school, your teacher taught you not to write the same thing twice, not to use the same word twice when you might instead be able to use a synonym. I suspect that this is why Americans tend to say "extremely" instead of "very" so very – er, *extremely* often.

In training, however, originality is often a bad thing. If you use different words in different places to describe the same thing, you may confuse learners into thinking that you are actually talking about two different things.

So, within one training document, you can use autotext and even simple copy-and-paste procedures to keep your wording standard. You can also use one document as the basis for another, not only in terms of templates, but also in terms of the content.

But what about when you have a library, or even several libraries, of training documentation? After a while, it becomes unwieldy to manage content manually.

Content management systems exist for this reason. The idea, much like software programming objects, is to atomize your training documentation. That is, instead of thinking of training documents with pages of text, begin thinking of discrete, small pieces of text that are directly tied to a very particular subject. Those pieces of text can be reused in multiple places in the same document, and they can be reused in other documents as well. Text that you write once can, in theory at least, be reused more or less seamlessly in a student workbook, an instructor guide, and online learning modules.

There is obviously a great deal of thought and work involved in planning a document using a CMS, because the structure of the document becomes an essential part of the document. You have to think of the text pieces you will need, whether they exist already or need to be written, and how to write them so that they can be reused in multiple formats and documents. The effort becomes cost-effective as your document library grows.

In the old system, you know that you can reuse content from a previous course for a new one, so you copy the hundreds of pages from that course over to your new working folder for the current course. And then you start the work of combing through those pages to see what needs to be changed.

The obvious stuff includes the customer name – though the fact that this is obvious does not mean that courses do not sometimes go out with the wrong customer's name on them! But beyond that: say the new project is indeed similar to the old one, but with a number of significant differences, too. Maybe the old course included five of your company's products, while the new one includes three of those and one that was not included in the old course. You now have to check the entire course to make sure that it does not reference a product that won't be part of the new course.

Now imagine putting together a course using a CMS. Yes, there will still be new development for your team to do, and some rewriting. But you may save a significant amount of effort by using your CMS to call up the relevant text and graphic objects into your new course, and each of these will, at least in theory, be written in such a way that you shouldn't have to rewrite them.

The key thing for you to know as a manager is this: it can be a natural tendency of your trainers to want the coolest tools. It's your job to evaluate, on a dollars and cents basis, which tools will enable your team to produce what it needs to, in the context of your company or organization, at the lowest cost. So when you evaluate whether you need a CMS, and if so, which one, keep in mind that the best system may not be best for you. That goes for content management, and it goes for all the other tools your team needs: simulation software, graphics software, computer hardware, and all the rest.

Chapter 9
Estimating, tracking, and managing training projects

Determine the project scope

There are two elements involved in determining the scope of a training project. One of these is in your control: your professional estimate of the work required. But the other may be quite out of your control. Your customer, whether internal or external, may simply dictate that they want a five-day course because Marketing or some other power-that-is thinks that will be about right, or they have a budget of 1.5 person-months, or a timeline of three weeks, and you can spend from now until eternity trying to argue the question, but it won't help you get them to budge from these predefined constraints.

These external criteria – external, that is, to your process – are not necessarily an enemy. In some organizations, they are dictated to the training department for no better reason than because the trainers do not track and estimate their own projects. This is something you can change, as of right now, as you begin to quickly take control of your own estimates.

Even if your organizational structure is such that you are not free to officially estimate your own projects – hard as that is to imagine, and even harder to defend – that need not stop you from providing your customer or boss with your own figures to compare with their own. You can establish a professional reputation for your group if you're able to provide accurate, detailed estimates based on your own group's track record. Even if these are not the official estimates for the project, they will carry more and more weight if you do them correctly. And it is possible that you will find yourself getting asked for estimates, or to check provided estimates, earlier in the project lifecycle as a result.

Estimates and schedules

So how do you estimate with accuracy? Is it really just hunches and guesses plus a fudge factor of "double whatever your guess is"? (In project planning terms, that would be assigning a contingency of 100%, which for most projects would be wildly unacceptable.)

Thankfully, the answer is that you can indeed create reliable estimates with greater and greater accuracy as you go along. You do need fudge factors (which you will call "contingency factors" when you show your estimate to anyone else, so that they will come away suitably impressed with your professionalism) and you do need to make clear what's in scope for your estimate and what isn't, and so on. But first start with the estimate itself.

Define the deliverable and its scope

You need to define the deliverable – at least a first take at what your actual output will be. Have a look at the system, find out at least the basic information on the audience, and whatever base documentation exists. Talk to developers, read the brochures, the design specs if they exist, and whatever else you can lay your hands on. Your goal in this step is not to establish that you will be writing a 217-page student workbook with 42 screen shots. Your goal is to get a sense for the scope of the deliverable you are being called upon to produce. How big is the system or product that is to be documented? How complicated is it? What information and human resources will be available to you in the form of SMEs? Is it similar in nature or scope to other projects your team has done? How informed is the intended audience?

With these basic parameters established, even if not precisely quantified, you can proceed to the next step: creating an outline.

Create an outline

Use this information to build an outline – yes, an outline – of your course or whatever it is you are to produce. Sure, some things (a lot, actually) will change later. But your goal at this stage is to get the best picture you can of what you will actually produce. Bring the outline down to the lowest level of detail that you can. When you are creating training, you should generally organize your course around user tasks, so ideally each discrete task will have its own topic in your outline.

So now you know something like this:

- Chapter 1
    - Topic A
    - Topic B
- Chapter 2
    - Topic C
    - Topic D

and so on.

Analyze the topics

Next, look at each topic in your outline. Estimate how many pages it will take you to cover each one, including screen captures and everything else. You can do this if you've broken down the outline into manageable topics. Admittedly, this will be harder for you when you first start estimating projects. But it will become easier with practice. You will quickly be able to recognize topics that are small, medium, or large, and for estimating purposes, that's usually all the level of detail that you need. And you can also compare the complexity of new topics to topics you have done in previous projects; if it's a similar size, you can do a lot worse than using the page count from that previous project's workbook.

For example, say that in your group's course documents, a small topic can be covered in three pages, a medium topic takes five, and a large one takes seven. (Remember, you already broke down the outline into the greatest possible division of topics, so the topics themselves should be relatively manageable in size – not only does this make your estimating easier and more accurate, it will also tend to improve readability and usability of your document by the user.)

Go through your outline, and for each topic, define the topic as small, medium, or large. Remember, this is an estimate, and does not involve mortgaging your children if you are wrong. By estimating each topic separately, you improve your overall chances at making accurate estimates, because you can reasonably expect to underestimate some and overestimate others, and the two should more or less cancel each out if you don't have an overly optimistic or pessimistic approach.

So now you know something like this, for each of the elements in the outline you previously created, showing all the topics to train:

- Chapter 1
    - Topic A – medium (5 pages)
    - Topic B – small (3 pages)
- Chapter 2
    - Topic C – large (7 pages)
    - Topic D – medium (5 pages)

and so on. You have the estimated page count for each and every topic that you have identified that needs to go into your document. Add them up, and you have the estimated total page count for your student workbook. It sounds low-tech, and it is. It also works, provided that you do a reasonably good job of estimating which topics are large, medium, and small. You can even add an extra-large category if you like; say, 10 pages, though it is likely that past a certain size, you should consider breaking down a topic into smaller pieces.

The more atomic you can make each piece, the more accurate your estimates are likely to be, because the scope of each topic will be clearer as you boil it down to size. To illustrate this point, consider the opposite extreme, where instead of breaking down your document into discrete topics, you try to estimate the whole thing all at once. You could easily be off by 30 or 50 percent, because at that level of non-granularity, you will not be able to see how big your project really is. By breaking the topics down as much as you reasonably can, you can estimate each one with a good amount of accuracy, because the margin of error for each will be relatively small.

Are you concerned that the small errors in estimating each task will add up to an enormously large error for the total? You needn't be, because your errors in estimating are likely to cancel each other out. There will be some topics that you overestimate, and others that you underestimate. Unless you are a pathological optimist or pessimist, the increased granularity will give you a very good bottom-up approach to building a credible estimate that you can have confidence in.

Define a multiplier for your work: how many hours does it take you to write a page?

Next, you need to come up with a metric, a multiplier, to use in figuring how long it will take you to write those pages. There are so-called industry standards. But you will do better if you can be more precise, based on your own work environment and all that it includes – your trainers, your deliverables, your SMEs, the system itself, and so on. You can even define different multipliers for the different kinds of deliverables you produce.

You really can define the multiplier for your work, and except for the first project you estimate, there's no need to use an industry standard that may have little bearing on the reality of your work environment.

Think back to the projects you've done before, and try to determine what your average is for hours/page. And yes, do use an average. Some projects are more complex than others. What you want to do is get that average, which you can then further manipulate as necessary.

So if you know that Course X had a student workbook of 100 pages and you worked on it for 2 months (say, 360 hours), your hours/page metric is 360/100, or 3.6. It takes you, or it took you, an average of 3.6 work hours to produce each page of that document. That's a metric that you can use, and it's a defensible one, because it is based on reality: not the vague reality of a number someone else defined, but the precise reality of the work you do in your organization, in much the same environment as the next project you will do.

It should be clear that the more projects you track over time, the more refined your estimating will become, because the sample size will increase. In fact, your estimating abilities will quickly improve beyond what you might expect from an increased sample size if you add each new project's actual results back into your estimating formula to keep refining it iteratively as well.

You probably do not want to give out your group's average per page statistics to others, who will likely say, "Four hours a page?! I can write *ten* pages in one hour, let alone four!" without realizing that these hours include research time, meetings, writing and answering emails, working through system crashes, and everything else that makes up the reality of work in your organization.

Still, it is good for you to know what your average is. That way, when you are in an interdepartmental meeting with other managers and the discussion turns to a new product and what it would cost to produce it, you can offhandedly toss out information like this: "Depending on the specifics, the Training group could produce a complete set of training for this project in about 11 person-months." That shows that you understand the same business language that your colleagues in software development do, that like them, you track and estimate your projects, and that the work of your group can be taken seriously.

Do the math: create a rough estimate for your project

Now that you know how many pages, roughly, that you will need to write, and now that you know what your multiplier is – that is, how many hours it has taken your group in the past to write similar pages – building a first, rough estimate is just a matter of doing the math. Multiply your average hours per page by the number of expected pages, and you have arrived at a first, rough estimate of the person-hours required for the current project.

Refine the estimate: build and iteratively refine an estimating formula that works

With the average in hand, you still need to produce a more refined estimate for the current project. To produce a more precise estimate for any given project, adjust your metric up or down based on your assessment of any special factors for that project. Keep in mind that every project has special factors; what you need to do to be as accurate as possible in estimating is identify what the significant factors for the coming project will be, and to evaluate them correctly.

Build your own formula; what works for me is a formula I made with the following basic factors for course development:

- Trainer ability and speed
- System size
- Scope of deliverables
- System availability and stability
- Quality and availability of specs
- SME availability and quality
- Rush factor

I use scales of 1-10 for each. (I have slightly different formulas for developing user documentation and for developing help.)

How do you build your formula? The answer is deceptively simple: analyze a past project, one that is already complete. If you have tracked the total number of hours (or months) that your team devoted to that project, do a little retrofitting of the data. (And if you haven't been doing this, start immediately!) Take the actual amount of hours/page from that project, and tweak your formula to adjust for the factors above, or any others specific to your work environment, until you have a formula that explains the difference between what a simple average across multiple projects would have predicted and that project's actual results.

If you can do this for several past projects, so much the better, because you will be constructing your formula from a larger sample size. Not only that: with at least a few projects under analysis, you will be able to see what caused one project to come in at 30% more hours than the average hours/page you might have expected from your other projects. Was it a different trainer? Was the system in an earlier stage of development? Were the SMEs less available or less helpful? Was it a rush job?

The point is that you must be able to identify the variables that add to your hours/page ratio for some projects and conversely subtract from it for others. There is no statistical or logical reason to assume that all of your projects will consume the same average number of hours per page; but there is no business reason why you should not be able to explain the variance of each project from the average.

So, to sum up: with an estimated page count, a metric for hours/page, and adjustments up or down based on the specifics for the project at hand, you can come up with a pretty good estimate almost all the time, usually within 10-15%. For projects that might be several hundred or thousand person-hours, that's a very reasonable degree of uncertainty.

Analyze completed projects to refine the formula still more

Some estimates will nonetheless turn out to be a little off. Even within that 10-15% margin, you want to be as precise as you can for next time. So you need to look back at the end of each project and figure out why it varied from what your customized formula with all the adjusted variables predicted.

In some cases, your formula was correct, just the data wasn't. For example, say your actual page count turned out higher or lower than your initial outline suggested. To correct for this in the future, look at the project data to see if your initial small/medium/large estimates were off. Maybe one of your team members has a tendency to under- or over-estimate the size of tasks. Or perhaps the project was a long one, and long projects may have more overhead time associated with them than short ones – more meetings, more managing, more emails, etc.

To automatically and iteratively refine your formula, keep modifying your hours/page metric based on the actual results from each project you do. Using spreadsheet software, you can easily build formulas in the spreadsheet that do this, so that the data from each completed project gets incorporated into the formula average. Your estimates should quickly become more and more accurate with this recursive formula.

Sounds like a lot of work, but it isn't as much as it sounds like, and the best thing is, it works. Internal and external customers will be very pleased when you can tell them with confidence that a project will take 2600 person-hours (yes, hours, even for large projects spanning more than a person-year), and they will be delighted when you deliver it for a little bit less, since you included a 10-15% contingency in your estimate.

Why it's important to use a formula

It's absolutely crucial for you to build estimates bottom-up in this way if you want to be accurate and to be taken seriously in your company. If you just used a thumb-in-the-air kind of method, you would very probably chronically underestimate. I know I would – I guess I just want to please or something. By forcing myself to go through the details, I eliminate that tendency for error. And, of course, pleasing people now with a low estimate that is not built on accurate data is in reality doing them no favor; that guesstimate will come back to haunt you as your team goes over the allotted budget of hours and time to get the project done. Try explaining then that you meant to please with that unrealistically low estimate.

Sample variables to use in your formula

Here are the actual variables I consider in my spreadsheet formula for training development. Some criteria are on a scale of 1-10, where 1 is the best possible and 10 is the worst. Others are on a scale with 0 as the midpoint, and either positive or negative values assigned; these criteria are used as multipliers for the base values to adjust them up or down as necessary. Different criteria have different weights based on our experience in past projects. I assigned the various relative weights by retrofitting the data to the actual history of completed projects, as described above.

- Trainer – how strong I think the trainer(s) on this project will be. This reflects both the trainer's usual abilities and any current considerations or distractions. If, for example, you have one trainer working on two projects part-time, he or she can't be as efficient as when working on a single project full-time.

- System size – how big, and how complex, is the system? There is, of course, no absolute standard to use for this variable. What counts is what systems are like in your organization, and how the present one compares with the usual – *for your company*.

- Product availability and quality – my teams typically created training for customized software when it was still in testing, so that we could deliver the training to our customers even before the release. This was important to the customers, because it meant that they could begin the work of building downstream training and documentation within their organizations using what we provided, even while recognizing that it might need tweaking after the actual release. In other cases, we would be directly training users so they would be ready for the conversion to the new system. The challenge for my teams was therefore greater, because it is harder to catch a moving target. Software still under development usually has bugs and always has features that have not yet been completed. Yet we, and perhaps you, need to document and train those features. So how well the system works when we have it is a major factor in building a decent estimate and getting a project done. If something hasn't been developed or debugged yet, your team has to apply time and creative methods to find a way to simulate it and train it, more time than would be needed if all were working as it eventually will.

- Specs and other docs – how available are they, and how helpful are they? You really don't need to run to the SME for every question about how a product or system is supposed to work, because the developers are supposed to create or modify the system to match the specifications. You can and should use specs and other documentation as a major input into your work, especially when you are at the initial phase of estimating the scope of each task. Therefore, the quality and availability of the specs is something you need to evaluate for the current project as you adjust your formula. If the specs are full and clearly written, great. If not, your team will be needing extra time to find the information they need, and this needs to be reflected in your estimates.

- SMEs – availability and quality. It is rare, at least in my experience, to have an available SME who doesn't know much, though it has happened. More likely is a SME who does know the product at least on a technical level (if not a functional level) but is not very available to your trainers because, as it happens, the SME is quite busy creating the product that your trainers need to train. Two points for a SME who is knowledgeable and available, at least within reason; one point for either.

- Rush factor – rush work is more complex, and though it may sound paradoxical, rush work also takes more time to produce. That is, it takes more effort, and so this needs to be accounted for in your estimate. Why is this so? Imagine a perfect work environment: your trainer has, set out before him or her, a perfectly working product to use in developing training, access to helpful SMEs with plenty of time, and all the rest. Now imagine the opposite: total chaos, looming deadlines that are impossible yet necessary to meet, and nobody has time for anything. Even if you were to control for all other factors in the other variables in this list, such as SME availability and quality, the rushed deadline itself introduces complexities into the formula. For example, you may have to throw several trainers at the task instead of having one trainer learn the ins and outs of the product and create the whole course armed with that knowledge. That will increase the need for coordination time and efforts among the trainers, the need for editing and quality control, and the need for your efforts in securing SME time for the trainers.

Take these criteria, and with the weightings you've given them in your formula, come up with a raw score for the project. Then multiply this raw score by your estimated page count (see above on breaking down the work into user tasks to do this) and by a running average of hours/page from all previous projects, and arrive at an estimate of the actual time for this project. Add a contingency factor of your choice (15% should be sufficient once you've established a solid base of project data in your estimates; at the beginning, you might want to use 25%), and you've got a detailed, bottom-up, reliable estimate based on real data for your internal or external customer.

How the formula helps you in internal and external sales

If you keep careful track of the actual hours spent on each project (so that you can continually refine your hours/page and, if need be, tweak the formula based on your experience), you can use this formula to arrive at very accurate estimates for new projects. With an accurate estimate, and a contingency factor to cover what even the formula can't predict (e.g. the SME got called to jury duty), you'll consistently come in under or at budget and make your customers happy.

Starting with this project, keep track of the number of hours you spend on each project, along with your measure of various criteria that make one project more difficult than another in your context. As your project history grows, you will have the numbers *in your company's context* for how long projects should take, on average. You can then estimate any future project by plugging the numbers into your ever-increasingly accurate formula as more projects get added to your database. Your managers will, I think, respond more to your numbers, since they will be based on *your* experience, than something you get from a book or a web site.

If you're in a quick-and-dirty kind of work environment, and you are pressed for a ballpark estimate in a meeting, you can use your formula to say that while every project goes through your team's bottom-up, detailed analysis in order to produce an accurate estimate, on average, your team – or better, your *company* – produces, say, a complete course with a 100-page student workbook in 2 person-months, (that's about 3.5 hours/page) or whatever your actual average turns out to be. You don't have to say at that meeting that the theoretical project being discussed will need precisely 100 pages, because you don't know yet how many it will need. What you can say is that if this project is similar in scope to another one your team recently did (a sample copy of which you might casually show or pass around just to let managers see the kinds of work your group can do), then the work effort would be similar.

Estimates as input to project plans

When you are ready to go beyond your carefully produced and refined estimate into a project schedule, use your favorite project planning software, and plug in the required effort (that's from the estimate you just made) and resources for each task, mix in any constraints (like vacations, holidays, partial availability of resources due to other projects, whatever), and you'll get the expected duration. This will show you any immediate problems in the work schedule; perhaps you need to assign more personnel to the project to bring down the duration, and you will need to get approval for the added cost.

Estimates as input to pricing

Finally, as to pricing, most relevant to you if you run your own training agency, but possibly also relevant if you are a manager in a company that bills per project, you need to come up with pricing. Customers sometimes prefer a fixed price for projects, so they know what the whole thing will cost, and may be willing to pay a premium for this security over what they might pay at a straight hourly rate. You, of course, don't want to get stuck by underestimating the project. So, using your detailed, accurate estimates, add an increased contingency factor above what you would normally add, just to make sure that your costs are covered. If you normally use a 20% contingency factor, you might want to bump that up to 30% in a fixed-price scenario to cover the added risk of a fixed price.

Assemble the project team

Okay, now you have reliably estimated a project and made the sale, whether internally or externally. Like first-time parents taking their newborn baby home from the hospital, the realization dawns on you that suddenly you have a *project* to do. Not only are you responsible for getting the project done; you even have to find the people to do it.

There are four basic possibilities for sourcing the human resources you will need for your project:

- deploying existing internal staff trainers
- deploying existing staff trainers from another group in your organization
- augmenting your staff with contract trainers

- augmenting your staff with permanent new hires

Deploying existing internal staff

Perhaps the simplest in logical terms, though not necessarily so in reality, is to have a large enough team, or a flexible enough delivery schedule, that you can just assign the new work to the dedicated members of your existing training team.

This simplicity in theory does not always exist in reality. It's rare to find an organization where trainers can sit on the bench in between projects for any length of time, waiting for the next project to come their way in a state of availability. It may be rarer still to be able to time your projects so perfectly that, without such bench time, trainers are able to finish one project on a Friday afternoon and start the next on the following Monday morning.

But if the project schedules include some flexibility, then you may well be able to juggle your team between projects. Say the old project winds down a bit more gradually, as projects sometimes do: instead of neatly finishing on that Friday afternoon, it demands less of your trainer's time, perhaps 50% and then dwindling down gradually to 10%. That means that the trainer can begin on the new project at half time and build up gradually to 90% and beyond. That's a very realistic scenario in a lot of organizations, and while it requires some deft resource management on your part, it enables you to get more projects done with a finite number of trainers on staff.

Another way to manage the transitions between projects is to have ongoing work for your trainers to keep busy with during downtime. Say, for example, that your team works on a billable hour basis on customer projects. What happens in between projects? While such an organization will likely loathe downtime, because it is nonbillable, the best you can do may be to minimize it, with no expectation that you will actually be able to eliminate it altogether unless your team is severely understaffed.

In this case, you may be able to use the downtime between projects for training your team, for approved nonbillable training work – perhaps internal company training, or to lend your trainers to other teams in your company. And that brings us to the next option, though in reverse: borrowing trainers from other teams in the company.

Deploying existing staff trainers from another group in your organization

In some larger organizations, there are multiple training groups. For example, training may be distributed among company divisions or locations, or there may be trainers working in the Marketing or Product Development groups as well as the Customer Training group. In a pinch, you may even be able to use other available employees as trainers, depending on their skill sets.

If you are able, it is an exceptionally useful practice to establish an informal borrowing relationship with the other training managers, where you can each borrow trainers from the other when they are available. This is good for all concerned, especially in billable environments, because it greatly reduces trainer downtime while avoiding or reducing the need to hire more trainers. Of course, it is not always going to be the case that your need for two additional trainers for six weeks each will perfectly coincide with another department's having downtime of precisely that duration and those start/end dates. But there can be enough overlap that, with goodwill, you can work with your manager peers to improve the company's utilization of its training resources for the benefit of all departments.

When you borrow trainers from another department in the company, be cognizant of differences in content and style among the departments. You can't expect a sales trainer who has only worked on training reps how to overcome customer objections to jump into the techiest of technical training unaided, or vice versa. It will take an extra effort on your part to give them the rapid training they need to be able to do the work, and you must plan for this in the allocation of your own time as well as of theirs. Also, in your estimating spreadsheet, take into account these varying levels of familiarity with your group's training process. Different trainers in your group will always have different productivity levels, and all the more so when you deputize trainers from another group into yours for temporary assignments.

Deploying trainers from elsewhere in your organization is thus not without costs and risks. But these costs and risks may be lower overall for your company than bringing in new trainers from outside the organization altogether, and may in some cases also lead to cross-pollination among training teams. Knowledge shared across company silos is a good thing.

Augmenting your staff with contract trainers

The next option to augment your staff for a particular project is to turn to contract trainers, who will normally be experienced and ready to start producing quickly. What contract trainers specialize in, in addition to any vertical industry knowledge they bring, is hitting the ground running.

The drawbacks are that they will of course not be familiar with your company and its products, nor with your group's style and how you do things in general. But the pros among them will be willing to bring general expertise in the art of training – specifically, of wringing information when necessary out of the minds of the SMEs in order to create what needs to be created – and will usually be quite familiar with the use of the standard software and other tools that trainers use. They may even help you automate some processes with their application of knowledge of the tools.

Good contract trainers usually cost money. Bad ones – journeymen who bounce from project to project because they can't hold down a regular gig – can be very hazardous to the budgetary and deliverable health of your project.

To find a good contract trainer, you can use an agency. But this often brings far more in the way of added costs (the agency's markup) than any assurance of greater quality of the trainer. It can be better to use your own network to find the contract trainers you need. Start with your own staff, and ask who they know. If you already have some contractors on board, ask them who they have worked with and recommend.

If your budget is limited, one option to consider is hiring inexperienced contract trainers, including recent college graduates. Paradoxical as this may seem, new trainers who have not become jaded or learned bad work habits can be an excellent addition to your team. If you can find intelligent, diligent people with good aptitude, you can quickly train them to produce what you need, and at a lower hourly rate than someone with years of experience. A variation of this option is to build teams consisting of both veteran and new trainers, to get the most out of both ends of the experience spectrum.

Augmenting your staff with permanent new hires

The last of the four options is to hire more permanent trainers for your team. The advantage here is that the relationship will, hopefully, be a long-term investment on both parts. The new trainers will not only learn your products, tools, and methodologies, but they will also carry this knowledge and build upon it for future projects that they will do on your team. There will be less wheel-reinventing, and if you are chronically understaffed, additional permanent members of the team will make sense. Over time, they can become valuable team members, and grow into team leadership roles and beyond.

The hiring of new permanent trainers for your team should not be done lightly. Unlike borrowed members of other teams in your company, and unlike contractors who can be fired at a moment's notice, if a permanent hire does not work out, the issues are more complex, at least in the United States. To fire a permanent employee often requires copious documentation of performance improvement plans and the communications thereof, all in conjunction with your HR department to avoid illegalities or exposing your company to the possibility of legal action in an extraordinarily litigious society.

One way to mitigate the risks of hiring new permanent employees is to bring them on for a trial period of several months, or even to start them off as contractors. (And if you use agencies to find your contractors, or even just to bill for them, make sure you put an option into your contract with the agency allowing you to hire any of those contractors on a permanent basis.) These variants of the permanent hire option will allow you to get to know the new trainers and their work, how well they work with the team and the organization, how diligent they are, and whatever other criteria are relevant for the work your organization does. See Chapter 7, *How to hire trainers*, for more information on hiring.

Writing a staffing plan

In some organizations, you may be required to write a staffing plan, a document setting out your anticipated staffing needs for known and, to some extent, not yet known upcoming projects. This is especially helpful as you consult with your management about the optimal combination of the staffing options described above: they will be able to see what is in the pipeline and how you propose to deal with it.

To write a staffing plan, you will have already estimated the work for each project in the pipeline, and you should also have estimated the probability of each project coming to fruition. In some organizations, this probability will be a murkier number than others, and you should note this, along with any known dependencies affecting project award.

So, armed with the knowledge of the *maximum* number of people you will need if all of the projects happen (keeping in mind that some may overlap), and also various estimates of the *probable* numbers – using the resource estimate for each project multiplied by the probability that you will be awarded that project, isolating individual projects from the total so that you can discuss each, you can write your staffing plan with an intelligent discussion of the various scenarios.

It's unlikely that all of the projects will happen, and even if they did, you will likely be able to smooth out the resource requirements curve by spreading the projects out over time. Look on the curve for the peak resource needs; if they are of relatively short duration (perhaps anything less than a year), that's probably an indication that you should be looking at one of the temporary staffing solutions described above (borrowing resources from other departments or hiring contract trainers).

If the curve remains high for an extended period, that may be an indication of a need for more permanent staff, provided that the projects are of a sufficiently high probability of being awarded. You don't want to hire a bunch of people and then not have work for them, and the hiring process in most organizations takes a lot longer than it takes to bring on contractors.

In other words, you do not generally want to staff for the peaks in your plan, but for a point on a curve that will cover most of your needs most of the time. You can manage the overages through other means: spreading projects more evenly over the time period in question, borrowing resources as needed, prioritizing projects, establishing phased approaches for projects instead of doing them all at once, and so on, based on what is realistic and acceptable in your organization's environment. If your company is especially conservative in its resource planning when it comes to permanent hires, you'll adjust the point downward on the curve to reduce or even eliminate any foreseen bench time. This will require, of course, greater use of the various temporary staffing solutions.

Remember that probability is a nice thing, but while you can use it as a tool in predicting, you should not rely on it to blithely go out and hire a precise number of resources. Your project visibility will almost always be somewhat limited – weeks or months, but often not much after that. Unless you have a pipeline of committed projects that you can take to the bank, tread carefully in your treatment of the options in your staffing plan. It is always easier to hire more people if needed than the reverse.

Provide resources and leadership

With the team in place – which in many projects need not happen all at once, but instead with various team members joining at various times as needed and as available – how do you manage the project to success? What do you need to do?

The primary role of a manager during a project is to help the members of the team do what they need to do. In some cases, this means that you will need to train them, or arrange for someone else (or various *someones* else) to train them in your tools, content, and methodologies. In some cases, this means getting them the time they need with SMEs who are busy and not being responsive. In some cases, this means getting them the tools they need to be productive – a cubicle, software, hardware, paper clips, or whatever it takes. Don't underestimate the effort required in these endeavors on your part – in a fast-paced, lean, or just hectic environment, even finding free cubicle space can be a real challenge. You may have to negotiate with other teams and your facilities team, or even find external space for your trainers if none is available internally.

Sometimes the resource that trainers need most is your leadership in helping them get the job done. If you see that a trainer is struggling to get started or is not staying on track, the worst possible course of action for you to take would be to wait it out, let them fail, cause the project to fail, and then nail them at the next evaluation time. By then, you will both have failed in your tasks, and *you* should be nailed as well at your next evaluation for letting your project fail when you could have intervened.

Instead, open your office door – in fact, keep it open except when privacy is needed – and walk around your team's area. Drop in often, even once or twice (or more!) a day, to check in with each trainer. You could get some, but likely not all, of the same information in a written weekly report from your trainers, except that they would have to spend precious time filling out some onerous report form instead of getting work done, and if they have a problem on Tuesday, you won't find out about it until the next Monday's report.

In reality, this dropping in is essentially a daily meeting with each trainer. But you will get more information, and more valuable information, by keeping it informal and oral instead of formal and written. When you drop in, make a note of what the trainers are doing. It's not your purpose to surprise them in order to catch them off-guard, and if company policy allows it, it's fine for a trainer to be making a reasonably quick personal call or using the Internet to look something up, and it's usually fine for trainers to be chatting with each other some of the time. The time you let them invest in building camaraderie will pay off when it's crunch time and everyone has to pitch in to help get the project out the door. It's also okay for you to join in a reasonable amount of chat and banter. These are your colleagues, if not your peers, and allowing people to be human is part of effective personnel management.

However, if things get out of hand, these drop-in visits will probably by themselves put a damper on inappropriate use of time. Knowing that the boss drops in has an effect. And if someone really doesn't get the point, you can bring the issue up right then and there, by telling the trainer that they need to reduce or remove distractions so that they can get the work done that you're paying them to do. (I once managed a project where we had to staff up extraordinarily quickly, and I relied on the recommendation of one of my contract trainers to bring on another contractor sight unseen. The guy was a decent trainer, but a pathological talker. The first trainer would periodically tell him to shut up, in so many words, and it worked, with no one taking offense. Good thing I didn't have to say that!)

The main purpose, however, of checking in with your trainers frequently is not to check up on them in any adversarial sense, but to see how they are progressing and to find out what obstacles, if any, are holding them up. A trainer may, for example, be having issues with unstable versions of the software under development. If so, you can help by arranging with the SMEs for access to both the current version – the one where the latest changes are being introduced – and the previous software version, which will not have the latest changes but may be more stable. The trainer can then switch back and forth between versions, as needed, to keep progressing on the tasks to be documented, instead of being stuck.

Probably the most frequent obstacle facing trainers is lack of SME availability. Without the subject matter expert being available to answer questions and explain functionality, the trainer may be stymied. You can help mitigate, if not resolve, this issue in a number of ways, ranging from a heavy-handed call up the company's escalation ladder to demand SME time (not usually recommended except as a last resort), to working out an arrangement with the SME or the SME's direct manager that might include defining the preferred communication method for the SME – perhaps email questions, perhaps drafts with embedded questions inside – or identification of an alternate SME with at least some knowledge in the subject area, any of which will help your trainer make progress even while not a perfect solution.

Yet another way in which you can help is by serving as an alternate SME yourself. You should have enough knowledge of the products that your team trains to be able to do this at least at a basic level – and for some products, at a near-expert or expert level. You don't need or want to waste a SME's time with basic questions from your trainers. Instead, tackle them (the questions, that is, not the trainers) yourself. Your main job in this phase of the project is to keep your trainers progressing by removing obstacles from their path. Remember, their success and failure are yours as well, and will be seen as such in the company.

Working with outsourced trainers or outsourced SMEs

If you are working with outsourced trainers, your job as project manager takes on some new complexities. It is likely that you will not have even met some or all of the trainers working on your project, and even if you have, you are by definition not going to be in the same physical location as your team. You will not have the option of walking over to their cubicles to check in with them daily.

You will have to replace the face-to-face contact you have with local trainers through the communications methods available to you, including emails, phone calls, videoconferencing, webcams, instant messaging, department blogs and wikis, and whatever else you can come up with to try to achieve a similar result: staying in touch with your trainers daily, and preferably more often, to check on their progress and remove obstacles. It's likely that their access to SMEs will be even more limited than in an in-house setup, so your role in getting information to your trainers (even if they are not really "yours") becomes all the more important.

You will also need to manage the work of the outside trainers by establishing standards, managing development processes, tracking progress and deadlines, reviewing deliverables, maintaining ongoing communications with your management and peer departments, and all the rest. Even if the trainers work for another company, you are, in the eyes of your company, the manager of this team. Find out what your company defines as success in this new setup (and help define this, if you can, to include not just cost savings, but whatever else your customers really need), and manage to it.

A reverse scenario is also possible, where your trainers are in-house, but your developers are outsourced, or remotely sourced in another location. Your role as facilitator of your trainers' work in this situation is similar to when the trainers are outsourced, namely as information facilitator *extraordinaire*. In addition, there will likely be cultural and language barriers that you will have to find ways to reduce. Some of this reduction can come through the communications methods described above, and your team's work will also likely benefit from as many visits as the budget allows back and forth, if not for your whole team, then at least for you. Establishing a personal relationship with the remote team and your peer managers will solve a lot of problems later on, allowing you to solve problems and defuse tense situations before they blow up.

Track and report

One of the jobs of a project manager is to track the progress of each project and report upwards and laterally (and to your team members, too!), noting any issues, risks, and problems along with the more humdrum adherences to schedule.

Reporting to management

You need to report upwards to your management, giving them the information they need about your project and its status as a component in larger projects (e.g. training development and delivery as part of a software product delivery). If there are issues that you can see, you need to share them with your management so that they will not come as surprises to them later on. This allows your manager to help you mitigate the risks, whether that means reducing the scope, adding resources, extending deadlines, or other means.

Reporting to peers

You need to report laterally to your peers who are managing related projects. If yours is *the* training team, as it likely is in most organizations, your peers will be managers of the product team or teams, along with whatever other stakeholder groups there may be for a particular project. When you attend overall project meetings, this is when you will contribute information on your project's status.

Reporting to your team

And you need to keep information flowing constantly to your team members. There are managers who keep their team in the dark, operating on a "need to know" basis – and the result is rumor, suspicion, alienation, and – well, you get the picture. Far better for your team members to have a clear picture of the team's progress on the current project and other projects that your group is working on, as well as a clear picture of the status of the overall project and the company as a whole.

Project management software

How do you do this tracking and reporting? Where do you get the information from? You need both a means of tracking your progress and a means of reporting on that progress, along with any issues that come up.

Project management software can be very helpful in tracking anything beyond the simplest of projects.

Once you have five trainers working on three courses each in overlapping schedules as part of a larger project, with SMEs from different departments serving as information sources, along with an editor back in your group whose job is to review the work of each of the trainers' drafts, it's too much for you to keep track of in your head. If you have 20 trainers, all the more so.

Note that a "project" as defined in project management software is really only about the schedules, resources, tasks, dependencies, and milestones of your real-life project. Managing the project is more than managing its representation in software. But, having said that, if you are going to stay on top of the real-life project, you need the tools to track the details of progress so that any delays will make themselves apparent to you for follow-up. As projects grow in complexity, the importance of staying on top of your project's progress and any areas of delay or risk of delay will only grow. For this reason, you need to become very comfortable in the use of project management software.

Get yourself trained, or train yourself, on the project management software used in your company, and update your project plan constantly based on your walks around your team's work area. Input the information you get from your trainers of tasks completed and delays.

Training program communication

I've seen movies and webcasts featuring management explaining the strategic importance of both the training program and the system changes that were going in place with it, along with monthly glossy bulletins and all the rest for really big training initiatives. Depending on how big your project is in the context of your company, the communications strategy will need to be adjusted up or down. Your task in communicating the training program and its progress can make the difference between motivated learners who understand the importance of the training program and unmotivated learners who refuse to learn – and who can ruin it for everyone else (especially the instructor).

Sometimes the challenge is more acute with soft skills training. People generally understand that if there's a new system coming in, they have to learn it (though they may well not like it). If instead the training is on the latest biz buzzword that the CEO heard on the golf course, that's a high hurdle to overcome in motivating the class.

Deliver the project

After all the estimating, planning, staffing, and tracking…you need to actually deliver the project. Don't let the planning, necessary as it is, blind you from the need to produce the deliverables on time, on budget, and on quality. True, in some circumstances, one or more of those factors sometimes needs to be fudged a bit; if your training materials must accompany the product and the ship date is fixed, you will have to have your training as ready as it can be on that date – and hope for the best, along with the chance to send out updates as soon as they are ready.

But managing a project is more than tracking and reporting and mitigating. It's also *delivering* the deliverables. Versed as you must be in the details of your projects, remember to also focus on the big picture of what you need to produce, and on getting it out the door when required.

When deadlines loom, your team will need your support and the knowledge that they can count on each other. Especially if you need them to put in extra effort – and it goes without saying that if you need them to put in extra time – show them that you're in it with them. Don't wait to get a report the next morning that the midnight deadline was met (or not). Be there at midnight with your team. If you arrange for food and other logistical necessities as they work late into the night or on a weekend, your team members will appreciate it. If your project's successful delivery depends on a pizza delivery, so be it. And your presence in the trenches will be the single most powerful statement you can make about how much you care about your trainers, the work they produce, and your company. If you absent yourself, your team will get the converse message, and understandably so. Even if you're unavoidably away, meeting with customers or at another company location, stay in contact with your team, especially as crunch time draws near.

Evaluate the project

When the dust settles – when a project reaches its completion – it is tempting to never look back at it and simply to move on to the next one, which may already be behind schedule. But this is a mistake; resist that temptation. Don't just toss the new course binder on your shelf.

Depending on the size of your operation, it probably isn't necessary to conduct a lengthy, formal review of completed projects. But there are four things you definitely want to do for every single project.

Evaluate project stats

The first thing you must do is evaluate the statistics of your project: did you deliver on time? On budget? On quality, using agreed metrics? Your completed project plan will give you the on-time and on-budget information. Enter your project's final stats back in your estimating worksheet so that it will be added to the population of projects used recursively in calculating your team's average output.

Analyze variances from your estimates

There is another step here, too, of no less importance. If your recently completed project deviates significantly from what you estimated, you need to understand why this happened. Compare the actual numbers with your estimates for this project and find out what the causes were. Was the scope larger or smaller than estimated? Did a particular trainer go slower or faster than projected? Was the software less or more stable than you expected? You need to look at the details to understand the source of any significant deviation so that you will be even better able to estimate new projects to take into account whatever risk manifested itself in this one. If you can identify the actual causes, you can refine the estimating formula to be more realistic going forward. If you can't or don't identify the actual causes, all you can do is adjust your contingency factors upward going forward, which is far less desirable as a management approach.

Evaluate the human side of the project

The second major task in evaluating a project is a human evaluation. This need not be formal. At your next team meeting, arrange for refreshments – for a large and difficult project, a company-sponsored team dinner could be appropriate – and talk about the project's ups and downs with your team. Come prepared with the results of the first step, and be prepared to hear insights from your team that you can use to better plan future projects. If all went well, this meeting can be simply congratulatory for a job well done.

Communicate project results

The third step in evaluating projects is to communicate laterally to your peers and upwards to your management, with copies to your team members. It is okay to highlight the successful aspects of your project, though challenges are fair game, too. Point out to all concerned if you came in under budget, won customer accolades, overcame some external challenge or other, and so on. Word the congratulations not to yourself, but to your team and the wonderful SMEs who worked with them. By thanking others, you subtly (yet modestly, of course) take part in their success.

Chapter 10
Running a training business

Much of this book has been about managing a training group in a company or other organization. But there is another kind of training manager: managers, often owners, of training companies or agencies…whether those agencies consist of only the manager/trainer or multiple trainers working for the agency at multiple clients.

While most aspects of management will be similar, there are unique issues that independent training businesses must manage, primarily related to finding customers. General issues of running independent businesses are a subject to themselves, and there are many books available on topics such as billing, financing, and similar issues. This chapter aims to cover issues specific to training businesses.

Finding jobs

It's of obvious and critical importance, whether you're a solo contractor or the manager of a multi-trainer agency, to find jobs. Jobs produce revenue, and without revenue, you don't have a business.

Targeting companies to be your clients

If you are in this for the long run, the best though most difficult method is to find out who the potential hiring managers are at companies in your area. Yes, you will have to make cold calls, something that many people are uncomfortable doing.

Yet this is how business gets done. You don't need to call up companies and ask forlornly if maybe they have some training that needs doing, for cheap, and you're sorry to be taking up their time asking. Here is what you need to do instead:

Identify companies to target

Identify local companies that might have training needs, based on what they produce. Read the business section of your newspaper, read the help wanted ads – not only for trainer positions, but for others that indicate the likelihood of there being a training function in the same company. For instance, if you see a company hiring programmers, chances are they also need training. The fact that they are looking for programmers is also an indication that they are expanding and not in a hiring freeze. (Even in a hiring "freeze," a strong enough business case can get exceptions made in most companies, but why swim upstream when you don't have to?)

Research the companies. Using the companies' own web sites and simple Internet searches, you will often be able to find the contact information for the training managers. Or, if not, especially in smaller companies that may not yet have any trainers at all, you can find the contact details for managers who might either need trainers or know who does in the company.

Make initial contact: email

Send an email to the contacts, briefly present your company as a local provider of training services, and ask if they have training needs that you can help them with. Include a link to your web site; if you have a testimonials section, link directly to it. Explain in a sentence, at most two, how you have helped other companies produce training for their products.

Make the second contact: snail mail

Let a day or two go by, and if you haven't heard back, send them a snail mail package: a letter similar to the email (and mentioning it), a brochure, your business card, and a request for a meeting. Mention that you'll follow up with a phone call to set it up.

Managers get lots of e-mails, many of them spam. Managers are busy, and if you go the route of calling by telephone as a first step, you will have only a few seconds to overcome annoyance; after all, you've interrupted whatever they were doing. But a personally addressed letter – well, now, these days I think that would stand out. As a manager, I'd read it just for fun if nothing else, to put the sender through

Steve's Ironclad Rule of Initial Resume Screening: did they manage to put together a letter, resume (or brochure), and maybe some collateral material without any errors? (Surprisingly few did.) If it actually looked interesting and showed good writing, that was a bonus; if they actually seemed to have thought about what they could do, and what *we* did, and how the former might match the latter, I'd be on the phone to *them!*

Make the phone call

Now the time has come for you to make that phone call. By now, it's not entirely a cold call. The potential hiring manager will have seen your email and read your letter. Your name will now be known to him or her, and when you introduce yourself, chances are that you will be greeted familiarly: "Oh, yeah, I got your email." What follows will either be something like "No, we don't need your services, and stop bothering me, you creep" – that's actually worse than you're likely to ever get – or, some of the time, "Tell me more." Even if this is ten percent of the time, you now have a very hot lead for your business. See how a cold call can warm up?

Difficult as it may seem for you, reaching out to local businesses instead of waiting for someone to contact *you* is by far the most effective means of finding new customers, because not all customers know you, nor do all customers even know that they need training services. This process also works, with the appropriate modifications, for reaching out to old customers from whom you haven't heard for a while.

When HR is your client

Some companies erect fortresses with mile-high walls to "protect" their hiring managers from the outside world. Those walls, seemingly complete with turrets and machine-gun nests, are patrolled by HR.

This is a more difficult situation. Your best bet is to establish at least preliminary contact with the actual hiring managers, no matter what HR says. Generally speaking, HR is not the controlling force in most companies. If the engineers or whoever makes the actual product have a business need for some training, they will be able to make their case with management, if necessary, and get HR to do the detail work of doing the initial screening for the positions they (the engineering departments) create.

HR screeners are often not able to discern who is really qualified for a job or a contract gig. What they are able to do is search resumes for keywords. The hiring manager says she needs a trainer. The HR person asks what skills the trainer needs. The hiring manager says, "I think we use Word for our training documents. Or maybe FrameMaker." The HR person duly notes that the position requires advanced knowledge of Word and FrameMaker. Contrast this with the methodology of hiring trainers described in this book, and you see how HR, instead of being a helpful screener, can sometimes more or less just get in the way and ensure that unsuitable candidates get presented to the hiring manager.

Even so, especially if your potential client is a large company, you may have little choice, at some point in the process, of establishing a relationship with their HR department. If you're an individual trainer, chances are that they will simply direct you to an agency that they work with. If you're an agency angling for some of their training business, your first sale may have to be to HR, and it's even possible that your official relationship will be with them – never mind the fact that you and your trainers work day-to-day with the engineers or in-house trainers.

How do you sell to HR? Like any good business – like any good sale – you have to demonstrate value in the proposition. HR will want to know not only how good your trainers are – if they are even able to judge – but how good your processes are: how easy or hard will it be for them to work with you? How smooth is your billing process? What rates are you offering them? What record do you have in covering your trainers' employment issues? Do you have no-harassment policies in place? What about nondisclosure of client information – are your processes up to standard? Are you easy to reach in the event of problems or disputes? In short, are you professional enough to minimize their concerns about working with you? Make your case, and you can win some business. Or at least get past the HR entry gate into the company. Once you are an approved supplier, you can hunt for projects inside the company.

My experience is that HR people can tend to notice paper more than electrons – though this could be simply because in these electronic days, paper stands out. If *everyone* started sending paper, the effect could disappear. Also possible is that HR people, I believe, tend to be not technically-oriented, but people-oriented. Well, they're supposed to be, anyway. On the other hand, HR recruiters are used to doing keyword searches in Monster or Dice, so make sure that your resume, if you're a solo trainer, has a keyword section where you list every single piece of software you've ever worked with or on, along with industries, languages, business skills, and soft skills. The more keywords you have in your resume, the greater the chances that an automated HR screen will find you.

Solo contractors: writing your training resume

If you're a solo contractor, always write a cover letter to sell the hiring manager on reading the details in your resume. (That's the purpose of the cover letter, after all.) How do you do this? By summarizing in a few nicely-written points how *your* skills and experience meet what *they* need – and that you understand what this is, or at least have a pretty good idea what they need, by having done the research about them. Do your research on the companies you apply to.

And don't limit yourself to answering ads – just like agencies, who identify companies they want to target as clients, you, too, should be "hiring" clients instead of waiting for them to hire you.

As an individual, some of the tactics of identifying potential clients can apply to you. But for all but the smallest companies, it's more likely that you'll be working through an agency. Whether you do this or are able to establish a direct relationship with a client, your key marketing tool will be your resume.

Over time, I developed a 30-column spreadsheet to assess training candidates. (See the section on hiring in this book for details.) Three of the criteria are about resumes. Let's talk about them:

- Accurate and organized – as a document, a sample of your writing, is your resume scrupulously accurate, down to the smallest details, and organized in a clear and logical way (like a good training lesson)? Is the writing *really* good, so that it grabs the reader's attention without relying on empty buzzwords? Did you format it so that it looks clean and neat?

- Error-free – is your resume *absolutely*, without the *smallest* exception, free of typos, errors of fact, misspellings, and any other error that will proclaim to the reader, "I'm not really as careful about checking things as I'd like you to think"? In an exacting profession like training, hiring managers can expect you to be exact in your work – and certainly in your resume, which you, at least in theory, have all the time in the world to perfect and re-perfect.

- Proper tool use – did you format your document clumsily using spaces and extra carriage returns? Or were you able to use styles and other features of your authoring tool effectively and efficiently, as a mark of a pro? Does your document contain evident use of advanced tool use, such as macros or protection, to show that you really know how to get the most out of the tool?

Note that these are in addition to content. Don't let bad mechanics spoil an otherwise good resume.

Now, a word about content: remember that your resume is your initial sales opportunity. So sell! Keeping in mind all of the above – including the scrupulously accurate part – make your words show what you can do, based on what you have done. "Wrote a student workbook using Frame" doesn't tell a hiring manager much at all, especially if the manager doesn't even know what Frame is.

Why not instead say what you did to overcome the challenges of that project to deliver your course on time, on budget, to user acclaim, or whatever scrupulously accurate measures of success you can legitimately claim?

So don't focus on the tools. Mention them in their proper context, or perhaps in a Keywords section of your resume (so that automated scans will turn them up), but focus on what you got done. Show measurable, quantifiable achievements where you can. Show that you understand the business or scientific context in which you worked. There's nothing more valuable to a hiring manager, because this is a good indicator that you will understand a new business or scientific context if you get hired.

Training resume bloopers

Trainers ought to be great storytellers and also wedded to accuracy. Yet, since the best training is sometimes achieved through counterexample – that is, what *not* to do, I reproduce below some totally real examples of resume bloopers, plain mistakes, typos, bad writing, and strategic errors that crossed my desk as a hiring manager. All of these gems are real. The resumes in question went into the trash can. Don't do what these people did when *you* look for a job as a trainer!

- *"I have no writing experience at all,* **but I was born in Scotland**"

    Not only is it illegal in the US to base a hiring decision on a candidate's country of origin, provided that the candidate can legally work in the US, but the mere fact that the person was born in an English-speaking country was not much of a qualification at all – especially since she admitted that she had absolutely zero experience!

- *"I am **current** responsible for standardizing"*

    This candidate stayed current where he was, and was not considered for a job in my group, since he didn't know the difference between "current" (an adjective) and "currently" (an adverb).

- *"Able to set and meet goals in a **fast past** environment."*

    "Fast past" sounds nostalgic, at least. Presumably, the candidate meant "fast-paced." But since "past" is a legitimate word, the author's spell-checker would not have marked it. Nonetheless, in even a cursory proofread of the resume, this mistake would have jumped out, and the fact that it remained in this resume rendered this person's candidacy a non-starter.

- *"Computer **Base** Trainer"*

    The candidate probably meant "Computer-Based Trainer," someone who conducts training using computers. Instead, this made it sound like someone who trains using phone books to boost the monitor height by raising its base.

- *"Maintain 98% total quality accuracy."*

    This candidate evidently understood that quantifiable results are good to include on resumes, a point well-taken (and one made above). But in training, 98% accuracy is just not good enough. Imagine if cockpit training for airline pilots included inaccurate information "only" 2% of the time, or if your doctor slipped up in "only" 2 out of every 100 surgeries. In this case, the candidate's claim, bombastic as it was, was also insufficient. Moreover, no data of any kind were provided to back up the claim.

- *"Went to a seminar on software quality."*

While it's highly important to list pertinent achievements, attending a seminar for a few hours doesn't really impress. It didn't impress me, anyway. Vague, irrelevant accomplishments won't help in a resume. Also, "went to" is a weak phrase. A weak accomplishment weakly described; not what I wanted in a team member.

- *"[Name of company] is a company started by a **friend of mine**."*

The candidate was currently employed at a company owned by one of his friends. There are at least three problems here. First, being hired by a friend is not a very good indication of the candidate's talents. It's possible that the friend took pity on him when he needed a job.

Second, the candidate was still employed there at the time when he was looking for a better job. In other words, he was prepared to repay his friend's loyalty by jumping ship to a better position if he could find one. Of course, many job-seekers continue in their current place of employment until they find a better position, and then give notice.

But this situation was different: the candidate's boss was supposedly a friend.

Third, by unnecessarily calling the reader's attention – that is, the hiring manager's attention – to this less than flattering situation, the candidate showed poor judgement. If that candidate couldn't responsibly and persuasively present his work history in a resume, what would happen if I hired him and let him loose in meetings with SMEs?

- *"I am **superior** at ..."*

Resumes are not supposed to be where you practice your humility and modesty. But, still. "Superior"? Let the hiring manager judge how good you are based on your accomplishments, and tone down the self-accolades if you want your resume to do its job and get you an interview.

- *"I am interested in a position where I can develop a **synergistic relationship**."*

I guess it's okay to include buzzwords if you feel you must, as long as you don't overdo it, and as long as you use them correctly. In this case, the candidate claimed to want a "synergistic relationship" without specifying with what or whom. It didn't make any sense, and it didn't add any value to the resume.

- *"Developed **cirriculums**."*

  Never *mind* usage mistakes. Never *mind* grammar mistakes. Never *mind* bad writing. At least run a spell-check on your resume!

  When I saw this one, I enjoyed thinking that the trainer must have developed those "cirriculums" when she worked at the "circis."

When you craft your resume, please make sure it doesn't have any errors like these!

Training job sites

If you're a solo trainer, you should post your resume on relevant training job sites. Recruiters who need to fill a job req search these regularly, scanning for keywords to match their requirements. Update these online versions of your resume regularly; some trainers find that making regular updates to their resumes can bring them to the top of the listings returned in the recruiters' searches sorted by update date.

The reason why this is so is that many recruiters find that newly-posted or updated resumes are from candidates who are looking *now*, or at least actively, for a new position, as opposed to trainers who post their resumes just in case a sweetheart offer were to come their way or when their current contract ends in three months.

Along with web sites of all kinds, job sites come and go, but with that caveat, here are links to and comments on some of the most important trainer job sites. These include some of the large general boards and some small, trainer-specific ones. Remember to make sure your resume stays near the top of the electronic pile when a recruiter searches for a trainer by making frequent updates, even small ones, even daily.

- Monster.com (monster.com) – If you're looking for work, you should post your resume for free on what is probably the biggest job site on the net. In my experience, more recruiters look at resumes on Monster than anywhere else. You can also create automatic agents that will alert you of jobs that match your criteria. Don't be alarmed by the unlikely-sounding name of the site. On the other hand, while many recruiters use Monster, so do some less reputable outfits, and your resume here will get some spammish contacts as well as legitimate ones. Proceed with caution, and consider setting up an email address just for use on this site.

- Indeed.com (indeed.com) – one of my favorite job sites, because it is so very flexible and easy to use. Indeed aggregates job listings from many other sites, and while no one site can be your only source for job leads, Indeed is an excellent place to start a search. You can set up email alerts for the keywords of your choice, which can include companies, job titles, locations, or anything else that appears as text in job ads.

- Vault.com (vault.com) – Another job site, where you can post resumes, but also offers career information on lots of jobs and background information on specific companies. You can search for "trainer" or other jobs.

- Salary.com (salary.com) – Find out what you're worth (or what the market says you're worth, anyway!). You can use this in your present job when it comes time for that review, or in negotiating salary at a new job. Employers do this, especially at large companies, so it makes sense for you to have the same information. Sort of like checking the blue book before going car shopping.

- ASTD (astd.org) – If you pony up the membership fee, you can apply to the jobs listed at ASTD, the American Society for Training & Development, the largest organization of trainers. And you can also post your resume here, where hiring managers can see it. I recommend this site highly.

- Dice.com (dice.com) – An excellent IT job site, including many trainer positions. In my experience, posting your resume on Dice will lead to frequent contacts from recruiters who, again in my experience, seem to be looking to fill higher-level and especially more technical positions than some of the other sites, perhaps because they are used to looking for engineers and programmers.

- Clarity Consultants (clarityconsultants.com) – more on the training side of things, though also offering a number of technical writing opportunities, Clarity seems to focus on very high-end people and jobs: "The first choice of the Fortune 1000 for Corporate Training and Development Consultants." Clarity does traditional recruiting and also serves as an intermediary agency for independent contractors, helping find them work.

Jobs with training agencies

Most contract trainers work through agencies. If you know anything about relational databases, you'll understand why this is so: just as the way to solve the problems of "many-to-many" relationships between two tables is to create a third, intermediate table, routing the relationships through it so that they become manageable, so, too, with trainers and customers.

Like middlemen everywhere, agencies serve the customer, who needs trainers for a project but doesn't have access to a whole stable full of training talent. Contracts typically last from several weeks up to a year, so when the work is done, the contractors move on to another customer and another project. And agencies serve the trainers, because the trainers can focus on doing their jobs – developing and delivering training – while the agency goes out and finds the work, bills the customer, and provides benefits in various forms to the trainers.

Depending on the size of your local market, you may move from agency to agency as you go from contract gig to contract gig, or you might remain with one if it has sufficient work. This can allow you to accrue benefits in some cases.

Agencies and the IRS: whose employee are you?

There's more to the function of agencies than billing and paying salaries. In the United States, tax laws are such that customers need to be able to prove that contract trainers are not in fact their employees. If they were, the customers would be liable to the IRS for nonpayment of withholding taxes and the employer's share of FICA, Medicare, unemployment insurance, and other items.

It's a complex issue, with many different considerations used to determine whether someone is a contractor or employee, such as who determines work hours and location, etc. As a result of this complexity, and the natural desire of customers to avoid trouble with the IRS, the agencies offer a solution: they make the trainers the employees of the *agency*, so there is little doubt as to their status vis-à-vis the customer. In other words, if you're an employee of the agency, it's harder for the authorities to claim that you're really an employee of the customer. This gives customers peace of mind.

The agency business model

For this peace of mind, customers are willing to pay. Let's say you tell the agency you're willing to work for $50 per hour. The agency will then turn around and bill you to the customer at something like $75 to $100 per hour. Now, not all of that is the customer's peace-of-mind-from-the-IRS price premium. If you are the agency's employee, they have to do all the withholding and deducting that employers are required to do. They also bear the entrepreneurial risk of the arrangement: perhaps the customer won't pay the invoice on time or at all, or perhaps the trainer won't work out. They buy insurance, they advertise, they have an office with a receptionist and computers and a bookkeeper and a coffee machine, and all these things cost money. So a reasonable markup is both fair and to be expected.

Some agencies take on the entire training project. What they offer the customer then is a turnkey operation; they run the whole thing and actively manage the output of the trainers with an agency-supplied project manager, at a suitably larger price than when they act merely as the employer of record. Other agencies do nothing of the sort: all they do is bring you to the customer and handle the billing. Around holiday time, they send around little gifts to the relevant people in the customer's organization to thank them. And the trainers do the training.

Partly because of the whole IRS scare, which makes customers want to use agencies, and partly because the nature of the relationship rather lends itself to abuse, many customers will only work with designated "preferred vendors" – agencies that they have established a long-term relationship with. This is money in the bank for those agencies: the marketing is done, and from that point on, it's a gravy train. If you want to work for the customer as a contractor, you'll have to go through that agency. One rather forceful – and unabashed – trainer I once worked with negotiated a raise for herself when she told her agency that it was little more than a pimp operation, billing the client, paying her, and pocketing a very healthy difference. She got part of that difference in her own pocket as a result.

Alternative agencies

The agency business model described above is by far the most common. It works for all parties: the customers get their protection from the IRS (though perhaps this perception of protection is a bit exaggerated), the trainers get their contract work, and the agencies get a nice reward for their risks.

But there are also alternatives to this arrangement. Some contractors don't need a typical agency to find customers for them, because they either already have their own customers or know how to find them on their own. Still, the customers feel they need the legal protection of an agency, and do not want to engage the trainer's services directly on a 1099 (independent contractor) basis.

Enter the model of agencies serving as (minimal) employers of record. In this model, the contractor and the customer find each other on their own, which is another way of saying that the trainers do their own marketing. The parties then select an agency for the contractor to work through for the purposes of the project. The agency does not market the trainer's services. And most of the entrepreneurial risk is removed as well. This allows the agency to significantly reduce the fee it takes for providing a service. Of course, trainers never pay fees to an agency out of pocket. What this means is that the agency adds a smaller premium to the trainer's bill rate in the invoice to the customer or, alternatively, that the agency bills the client at the agreed rate, but deducts a small percentage as a fee when it pays the trainer.

Choosing an agency

First consider what kind of agency you need. If you're like most trainers, you may well need an agency to do all that icky marketing stuff and line up the jobs for you. What they make on top of your rate is of no concern to you – and indeed, they will not disclose it to you. If you go through what we'll call a full-service agency, all you need to do is pick a good one.

In some cases, this could mean answering an ad in the paper or on the net. You'll see agencies with ads proclaiming how they need trainers with these and those skills for a variety of projects. Often what that means is that they don't have anything right now, but want to build up their resume files, which is what they use to sell to customers. When they actually get a job req (requisition), *then* they'll start making calls to find the warm body to fill it. Such agencies – that is, agencies that advertise nonexistent gigs – are best avoided. What they do seems to me to be unethical and false advertising.

Probably a better way to choose an agency is to network with local trainers in your area who work with agencies. Find out who has a reputation for integrity – some do, some don't – who pays on time, who offers what services and benefits. Then approach the agencies yourself and make clear what your ground rules are. Common issues include trainer approval before the agency submits the trainer's resume anywhere, timely payment, and bench time (i.e. time between contracts). Ask around in your professional network for recommended agencies in your area.

Of course, it also happens – and this comes from experience – that agency recruiters call you if you have your resume posted on job sites. In that case, try to evaluate the position and the agency as fast as you can. If the offer is a good one, go for it. Contract work isn't indefinite, anyway, so how bad can it be? If you're currently on the bench, or will be soon, and a decent gig comes along for, say, three months, it may well be worth it to take it even at a slightly lower rate than you'd usually want. After that, you can move on to the next job…which you can be marketing yourself to all the while.

You might also consider one of the large consulting companies, which typically take on entire projects. If you're willing to travel relentlessly (typically every week, Monday to Friday or sometimes Sunday to Friday), this can be a great way to gain experience fast. But this may not be a lasting solution for you, because the business model of the consulting companies seems to be to get the most possible billable hours out of its (generally) young consultants until they burn out completely.

Finally, if you can find your own clients, but need an agency to be employer of record, you can either set up this sort of relationship with a full-service agency – something they're not often set up to do well – or go with an alternative agency.

Marketing yourself as a freelance trainer

If you're a freelancer/contract trainer, you need to promote yourself. Think of yourself as a store with exactly one product, namely your time (and if you are an agency with a stable of trainers, *their* time). You can only sell that product to one customer at a time. What you need to do is make sure that each sale is a good one, and that you sell as much of your time as possible at the best possible rate, because no one pays you for down time if you're independent.

In the old days, trainers may have gotten away without having to sell their services very much or very often. But more than ever, trainers and agencies need to sell to internal and external customers, and those sales have to be made on a value proposition.

Selling isn't really about the product or service at all, and you don't have to think that by engaging in sales you sully yourself. Good selling, what we might call healthy selling, is really about finding ways to meet your customers' needs. Sure, part of that process, once you demonstrate that you understand those needs, is proposing your way of meeting those needs. But it's only part of the process. And if you really can't meet a particular customer's needs, all parties, including you, will be better off if you see this in advance and make no secret of it; instead, you should try to come up with an alternative or two that will help your customer even if it does not bring revenue directly into your pocket.

This could include referring business to another trainer or agency with the necessary expertise or available resources, and working out a referral fee with them. Or it could include partnering with another organization to be able to meet the customer's requirements. Finally, it may mean simply declining the business if you just can't be of help.

Training is generally a service, and should usually be sold as such. How do you sell a service? Sell by demonstrating that you know what your customer needs, because you're an expert, and by demonstrating that you can perform that service efficiently enough that the value you provide will be greater than the cost.

But training can also be sold in the form of the products it produces. If you sell training as a product, you either create courses or other training products that go along with some other end-product. Once you have a good amount of experience in reliably estimating your projects, as described in another chapter of this book, you may want to charge per project instead of per hour – provided that you really are confident in your estimating abilities, and that you have the necessary provisions in your contract with the customer to handle shifting scope definitions and other contingencies. Without these, scope creep can quickly transform a profitable project into a losing proposition.

Creating and maintaining a training web site

Stores hang up signs, and some walk-in business comes their way. For a trainer, the equivalents include creating a web site as a sort of online resume. You can use this as something for potential clients to look at once you've established contact in some other way. Invite them to see your web site, and they will get an impression, hopefully good, of both your experience and your writing and design abilities. Make it easy for site visitors to contact you through mail, email, phone, social networks, and other means. Different customers will prefer different communications methods, so offer them all.

Once you have your web site up, keep it fresh with periodic updates, ideally every week or two. That will be of use both to human readers and to the search engines. Use appropriate keywords in your text. So, for example, if you provide sales training services in Manhattan, make sure that those words and variants of them appear in your text, in your headers, in the page titles and descriptions, and in links to your site from forums or ads. This can make a huge difference in the amount of traffic you get from the search engines.

One way to keep your site fresh is to include either an actual blog on it, or blog-like updates with comments on your business, your industry, your customers, and so on, provided that you reveal no proprietary information about either your business or your customers. Connect your blog to the social networks.

Before you consider how to promote your site – and certainly before you plunk down hundreds of dollars to get premium placement in search engines – consider what you are marketing in your site. If you are a one-person training shop, then it's not going to help you to engage in mass marketing to every potential client in North America. You've only got a fixed number of hours to sell. Imagine that you got to the #1 position for "training" in every search engine, and every single Fortune 500 company came to your door wanting to buy. Are you going to be able to sell your services to all of them? Probably not.

It seems to me that the marketing raison-d'être of a site for a solo training (or other) professional is not so much to gather in cold leads (though this does happen, and you should include an inquiry form for potential customers to use on your site), but to take warm leads and convert them into sales. Put your site on your cards, your resumes, your e-mails, etc. so that when people say, "Hmm, maybe this is the trainer (or agency) for me!" they are warmly invited to get to know your work better (including your specialties, experience, samples, location, etc.) at your site. When you make cold calls and emails to companies in your area that you want to sell to, give them your URL so they can check you out.

For this, you don't need premium placement, nor do you need any kind of high ranking on *general* search terms. (Specific search terms, as noted above, are very important!) Devoting money and even time to chasing a mass-market position in the search engines just isn't the way to promote a training business. Mass marketing is generally for products, not services, unless you have a national service business (like an auto body repair chain). You're usually going to be much better off pinpointing your desired market and going after it with outbound cold calls, letters, and networking.

The only exception I can think of offhand would be if you have an incredibly rare specialty. Let's say that you're one of 20 people in the country who are experts in a particular technology. Then the thing to do is create a good page on your site with lots of juicy info on that specialty. Give it time, and you'll start showing up when people search for that specific subject. If you want to jumpstart it, you could buy some keywords on search engines that target that highly specific specialty. But watch your search budget carefully – it's very easy to quickly build up a huge bill from paid searches, and the ROI can be doubtful in the extreme.

As an extension of their web presence, many businesses now also have a presence on social networks, such as Facebook, Twitter, LinkedIn, and others. Some customers will find you through these networks if you use them well, and you can also use the networks to reinforce your connections with existing and former customers. And new customers may find you if your existing customers "like" your company's page. More work-oriented networks such as LinkedIn may also be directly beneficial to you in finding new customers or, more correctly, in helping customers find you.

Designing your site

There are companies out there who will help you design a web site. But as a trainer, there's no reason you can't do it yourself (or at least with a very hands-on approach as you guide a designer into creating what you want). Find a domain (use your business name or as close to it as you can get) and a hosting service (best to keep these two purchases separate, so that you can easily move to a different host if the need arises), get yourself some web design software to do the work (using a template will do just fine unless you prefer to design by hand), and show the world what you can do.

Your goal in designing a web site like this is to think of it as an introductory brochure. Keep it professional, leave out the personal photos and the story about your dog, and keep the design simple and clean. Include testimonials, the industries you serve, possibly a sample or two to show what you can do, and whatever else you can think of that a potential customer would want to know about your company.

Remember that your primary audience will include people who don't know, and don't care, about the details of training tools that you've used. They've got business needs that they want to know if you can help them with. Tell them and show them how you solve problems for customers. Tell them what kinds of projects you can do. Since a web site is a brochure, not a resume, the projects you *can* do need not be limited to the projects you *have* done.

Samples and project summaries

What you want is a summary of the kinds of projects you can do. Put a few genericized samples on the site, leaving out client proprietary or identifying information, so visitors can get a suitable impression – but don't place entire or even partial actual projects there for the world to see and copy. Remember, your web site is just an introduction, not an encyclopedia, and you don't want to make it easy for competitors to download your work and pass it off as their own.

Customers don't expect to see complete samples of your work on the site; they just want to see examples of what you can do. Again, you can feel free to create samples as marketing materials, both on- and offline, even if their origin was not in actual projects. If a client asks if you've actually done precisely that sort of work before, you can and should answer honestly that your team created that sample to show your capabilities, whether or not previous clients happen to have purchased that particular product before.

Industry focus – identify your target market

If you focus on one or a few industries, highlight this very salient fact. Probably this is the single most important feature of your site, because visitors will be able to find you in search engines when they seek someone in that specialty.

Who knows, you might even help create some of your market in this way. Say someone is putting together a project on marine biology. They might not even know that they need a trainer. As they search for the relevant terms, your site comes up because it highlights your specialization in just that field. With a good site that explains how you can add value to such a project, the visitor will be on the phone to you soon enough.

E-mail as a marketing tool

With your web site will come an e-mail account (usually several, often unlimited). Use one of these as your professional e-mail – that is, with your own .com address, not a free email account from another provider, and include a signature with your site address and a one-line description of the services you provide. (Keep your personal e-mail separate; there's no need to tell Grandma about that marine biology specialty of yours every time you write to her.)

Business cards

Get some inexpensive business cards – they really don't cost much – with your contact info, including your web site address and the services you provide. Carry a few around wherever you go, because it happens that you meet people who will ask what you do. Give them a card, and business can sometimes result, even in unexpected ways. When you meet with potential clients, give them a card. When you send out something in the mail, include a card. Have cards in your office for visitors to take.

One inexpensive source for business cards is vistaprint.com – you can design a card online and get it printed and shipped for a very small amount. Pay a few extra dollars to get your own copy on the reverse of the card instead of their logo.

Active marketing techniques

You've got to go beyond the passive steps if you want to build up a business. You can't set up shop and wait for customers to beat a path to your door, because in most cases, they won't. The passive marketing techniques described above are all necessary, but most of them are backups, support or reinforcements if you will, to your active marketing plan. Marketing means figuring out who your target market is, what services you will offer that market, and the way to get to that market. If you're a one-person shop, as many trainers are, it's not that complex.

Identifying your core market

Say you've been working in the financial services industry, and actually know the difference between Series 7 and the World Series. Now you've decided to set up shop on your own as a contract trainer for financial companies. There's nothing wrong with taking on a customer from the automobile manufacturing industry and branching out, but this is not your first natural market. Your natural market is companies in financial services in your area. (Yes, you can get telecommuting work, but that's much harder.) So, make a list of the financial companies in your area. That's your core market.

Defining your services to the market

Now figure out what services you're going to offer this market. Let's say you want to focus on meeting this industry's constant need to update registered representatives with new product and regulatory information. Since the financial industry is a regulated one, there are specific rules for its communications to customers that must be followed, and the reps need to be given the information in the correct manner and with correct instructions so that they can work with their customers legally and correctly.

Contacting the market

The last step in this simple three-step process is to identify the people in the companies you've identified who may be in a position to buy your services. How can you do this? Here are some ideas:

- Network with other local trainers at your ASTD (American Society for Training & Development – astd.org) chapter meeting. Perhaps one of the members will know the training or other hiring manager – or one of them, if it's a large company. These networking contacts may be able to give you useful grapevine information, too, about what it's like to work at that company. You may not get much help from competing agencies, but if you're a solo trainer, other solo trainers will be more likely to help. You're not competition if there's plenty of work for multiple trainers. If you run an agency, individual trainers may still want to work with you and, while it's more likely going to be the case that you, not they, have contact information at the potential customers, you never know.

- Do an Internet search for terms like "learning," "training," and the name of the company. If they make a product that you can access, the training team contact info might be listed in the product.

- Call the main number for the company and ask to speak with the training manager. When you reach him or her, you've got about 10 seconds to make your pitch, so consider carefully what you want to say. In that amount of time, the manager will decide whether you are worth more time, and indeed, that should be the goal of the call: establishing a time and a channel for you to make your real pitch. If you happen to know that the customer is desperately seeking someone just like you, you can be direct. But in most cases, what you need to do is ask the manager if you can send a brochure and resume (or resumes, if you're an agency). Remember, you're interrupting whatever they were doing before, so now is not the time to talk unless they explicitly invite you to go into details. Send in the information, and the next time you call to follow up, you're practically old friends.

- Once you establish experience in your market, as each contract begins to draw to its natural end, you can reasonably market both inside that same company and outside. Say you just did a project for the company's sales team. When it's almost done, seek out other possible customers in the company. Perhaps there's a marketing team, a documentation team, etc. that could use your help. You can absolutely ask your direct customer to help in this search – provided that your work has been good!

Other marketing avenues

There are other ways to market your business in addition to the main ones described above. If you specialize in one or more industries, subscribe to the trade journals for those industries and consider advertising in them. Send press releases to those journals with newsworthy information about publications in that industry. If the material gets printed, you will garner free publicity for your company.

Consider attending relevant trade shows. Again, if you serve specialty industries, check out the possibility of attending their trade shows and meeting potential customers there. If you're a serious player in a particular industry, you might even sponsor a booth at the vendor portion of the show so that people can visit you, see demos of your services and products, sign up for free subscriptions to your company newsletter, drop their business cards in a bowl for a chance at winning a raffle, and so on.

You might sponsor an event in your own town, if you serve local businesses. For example, if there are startup companies in your area who have not yet reached the stage where they have their own training and documentation groups, host them at a free informational seminar on the importance of good training in achieving customer satisfaction, winning next-stage investments, etc. People like doing business with people they know, and your job as a marketer is to get to know lots of potential clients.

Managing your clients

Once you get clients – and that's the hardest part for any small business – you also have to manage those clients. It's an easy point to forget, if you're busy marketing and running current projects, but you also have to manage the relationship with clients, both those for whom you're currently doing a project and those for whom, at the moment, you're not.

The paper trail lifecycle of client management

The documents of the freelancing (or agency) business commonly include requests for proposal (RFPs), nondisclosure agreements, contracts, work orders, timesheets, and other documents. Let's consider them here in order of appearance in most projects.

Requests for proposal (RFPs) or requests for quote (RFQs)

If you're a solo trainer angling for work at a particular client, you'll probably never have to deal with such formal documents as RFPs or RFQs. But if you're an agency looking for five-, six-, or seven-figure contracts to provide training services to a large company, the first document in your relationship with that company may well be an RFP or RFQ.

The basic idea behind an RFP is that the customer knows in general what it needs, but the possible solutions may be complex and there may be a variety of ways that the solutions could be provided. In an RFP, the customer (or its consultant) will prepare a long list of requirements, ranging from business issues to ones. For example, you may be asked to detail your company's revenue history over the last several years, possibly including profit and loss information. The client wants to know this not just to be snoopy, but to get a sense of your financial stability. Clients do not want to risk dealing with a company that has little or no history, or a history of instability.

There is one absolute rule for answering RFPs: give the client what they ask for. This may seem obvious, but many companies lose contracts because they don't answer the questions that the clients ask in their RFPs. If you decide that you want the business, then answer each and every question in the RFP meticulously. If the client has taken the trouble to define a requirement, you have to take the trouble to answer with an explanation of whether you can meet that requirement at no additional cost, you can meet the requirement with modifications that would require additional cost, or you can't meet the requirement.

Obviously, you want most of your answers to be that your solution meets the requirement, but do not lie: if something will cost more, say so. And use the client's words in your answer. That is, even if you have a different terminology, or the client has chosen non-standard terms, use those terms. If the client asks for apples, and your solution talks about fruit, it may not be clear to the client that your solution actually addresses their problem. If they want apples, say apples. If you need to, describe how your solution includes apples, or whatever, as part of a larger, comprehensive solution, etc.

As part of this rule, follow the probably very detailed instructions on how exactly to formulate and format your answers. It's just plain foolish to lose a contract because you couldn't be bothered to follow the directions, including deadlines. After all, you're a trainer, aren't you? Gearing your materials toward the end goal should be a natural part of how you do business.

Usually, RFPs include a procedure for asking clarifying questions. Sometimes you can contact the client (or their RFP consultant, if they have hired one to manage the RFP process for them) directly; sometimes there is an open session for all bidders where the questions get answered for everyone's benefit. In some cases, this is done by email. The idea for making the playing field level is that the client wants to be able to objectively select the best vendor for the project, and this could be hard to do if the picture were muddied by favoritism.

Sometimes RFPs come with rather impossible deadlines. The client and their consultants have worked on the RFP for months and then, in their hurry to move forward, give respondents only a week or two to answer all of those detailed questions with answers that reflect detailed analysis and calculations. In this event, the client can sometimes be prevailed upon to issue a general extension for all bidders of perhaps another week or two, if enough respondents tell them that they need more time to prepare their proposals. Extensions are not generally given to only one vendor.

One proposal I worked on, submitted in I think three copies, weighed in at over 70 pounds when we boxed it up for shipping. That was back in the days when proposals had to be submitted as printouts; you may find that the majority of proposals today can be submitted electronically. Often this is now a requirement, because it makes for easier comparison of the various responses on a line-by-line basis or, as is common, row by row in a spreadsheet.

When you send in your response files, make sure that they are cleanly formatted and free of viruses (yes, I speak from experience! – back in the early days of PC viruses, we once sent a response to a customer who had already installed an anti-virus system. The company I worked for hadn't. Thankfully, the customer was very understanding, and allowed us to send new, clean files the next day.)

Also, again speaking from experience, if you use templates or reuse any text at all from previous proposals (after all, many of your proposals will have similar content addressing similar requirements from one customer to another), you must make positively sure that when you paste in that text, you change the customer name and any other relevant data in the current proposal. It just doesn't make a very strong selling case to say how proud you are of your tailored solution for customer X when you're actually delivering a proposal to customer Y, and all the more so if the two customers are competitors of each other in the same industry.

Not every request for a solution is complicated. Sometimes, if the requirements are straightforward, even standardized, the client issues not a request for proposals detailing the components of a solution, but a request for quotes (or quotations) that delineate the specified solution and ask only for pricing and general business terms in the response. RFQs are thus a lot easier to answer – provided that the underlying solution really is standard, which is not always the case – and naturally tend to focus more on pricing as a means of comparison than other elements that might play significant roles in a response to an RFP.

In your answers to any RFP or RFQ, remember that what you put in writing now will, if you get the contract award, become part of the contract, and you will be bound to it. Keep this in mind when you feel tempted to overpromise or underbid in order to win the project!

Nondisclosure agreements

These are legal agreements, usually mutual, where two parties agree to keep each other's confidential information confidential. Often, an NDA will accompany an RFP or RFQ; in other cases, it will precede them, if the RFP itself contains confidential information.

Most NDAs that I have seen are pretty standard. They require you to maintain the client's confidential information with the same care that you maintain your own, and prohibit you from disclosing it to any third party with the exception of answering any subpoenas or with regard to information that has been previously lawfully disclosed by someone else. You will probably be required to have your employees or contractors sign the NDA or an appendix to it as well, so that anyone having anything to do with the project will be included.

These are legal contracts, and so NDAs should be scrutinized and, if necessary, negotiated by your attorney. While, as noted, most NDAs are rather standard, sometimes a client's attorney will take things a little too far, and your attorney may want to negotiate any problematic language. For example, an NDA might also include a non-compete clause prohibiting you from ever serving anyone else in the industry, which would often be an unreasonable expectation. In such a case, get the NDA language fixed and agreed upon before you sign it. NDAs come with stiff financial penalties for violations, and you do not want to endanger yourself and your company unnecessarily.

Most NDAs are not problematic, and are part of the normal course of doing business. Read them carefully, and then in most cases you can sign them and get on with doing business.

Contracts

Congratulations – your proposal was the winning one, and now it's time to work on a contract with the client. Or, in a smaller project that doesn't require a formal proposal, you've won a new client and it's time for a contract. Don't start work on a project until you have a signed contract in hand. Even large companies sometimes make this mistake, and it comes back to haunt them to the tune of millions of dollars.

You should have a standard contract to use with your clients if they don't have one. This will often be the case with startups or other small businesses. Explain to your attorney what you need to protect your training business, and the lawyer will put together a contract with you. Don't be afraid to add your input, both to the wording and to the issues covered in the contract. For small clients, you can simply give them your standard contract, which is worded fairly but also not to your disadvantage, and have them sign.

Larger clients may have their own contract, and want you to use that as a basis. Remember, just because something is printed in a nice, official-looking document does not mean that it is engraved in stone. Don't worry about normal stuff. But absolutely go over the details of any client contract with your attorney to flag any issues that would be harmful or difficult for you. Negotiate these with the client so that the resulting final contract is fair and reasonable. Few companies are intent on forcing their business partners to sign unfair contracts, and even if their attorneys are a bit overzealous, they will follow the directions of the company's executives.

The basics of any contract with a client include descriptions of the kinds of services you will provide, how you will invoice the client, and the payment terms. Often, specifics of the project are left to a work order, which becomes an appendix to an overall contract.

You should also have contracts with your employees and contractors, setting out the respective rights and duties of both sides, including references to your company's nondiscrimination policies and policies prohibiting harassment, which you must have them sign, along with NDAs for your company and its customers. Even if you are a virtual shop and your contractors or employees never set foot in your office, you must have them sign these policies as part of your work with the clients they serve, who will require that you have such policies in place to protect them. If there is ever a violation or alleged violation of these policies, your defense rests largely on having put those policies into place and being able to show that the person in question signed a copy.

Work orders

It's usually convenient to have an overall contract with a client and then fill out specific work orders for each project and each trainer. Include the template for a work order as an appendix to the contract.

For example, if you have multiple projects with one client, whether simultaneous or sequentially, keeping the specifics of each project and trainer in a separate work order obviates the need to revise the contract and get attorney and executive approval every time a new trainer comes on board. Instead, for each new trainer, a work order is written to define the trainer's responsibilities (in general, such as "create training materials for the XYZ system"), client supervisor, and billing rate, per the contract. That makes it easy to issue work orders and get them approved by the client quickly so that work can start.

The work order is typically a short document, even one page, that briefly describes the project and sets out the billing rate for the trainer in question, the person on the client side whom the trainer will report to, and the timing of the project with start dates and end dates. General issues will have already been defined in the contract and don't need to be addressed or changed with each work order.

Another advantage of this separation is that, over time, you can adjust the billing rates of your trainers. On a first work order for a particular client, you might bill your trainer at $75; after a successful six-month project, now that the trainer understands the client's business in detail, it is legitimate to write a subsequent work order at a somewhat higher hourly rate.

Timesheets

Use any one of several inexpensive timeclock applications to track the billable and nonbillable time of your trainers, and issue timesheets (usually weekly) to the client in a format agreed upon in the contract. That might be a simple spreadsheet showing the trainers, their daily or weekly hours, the project or projects they worked on, and their bill rates. If a project involves multiple trainers, the client may want you to aggregate the individual time reportings into one summary. If your business grows enough to warrant it, you may need to invest in automating the process.

For hourly work, you get paid on the basis of the timesheets, so make sure that they are accurate…and make sure that you submit them on a timely basis.

Maintaining personal contact

Managing client relations is not only about paperwork. That can be hard to remember sometimes.

The fact is, though, that your clients are hiring you precisely because you're the one with the communication and explanation skills, and they might not have those particular skills. So while the paperwork is necessary, it's not enough. You have to meet with your clients regularly to monitor project progress, to build and maintain human relationships with them so that when things go wrong, as they will sooner or later in every project, there will be a basis of mutual understanding that you can build upon and draw upon in getting the problems fixed and the crises resolved.

So, show your face at the client's site – not unannounced, of course, but in coordination with your client contact. Let them see that you're not an absentee landlord, just hiring out your hired guns to make a tidy profit on each hour of their work. And let your trainers see you there, too, keeping tabs of how things are going in the project and for the trainers in general.

Invite your clients to an occasional lunch. Generally speaking, this won't be at white-tablecloth restaurants, or at least not necessarily, though also not fast food. The point is to show both a normal amount of hospitality and good management of funds – if you take a client to someplace really fancy, it's natural for them to wonder if they're in effect paying for this through your billing rate. They will understandably resent this particular cost of doing business.

Back at the office, keep in regular contact by email and phone with your clients. Your invoices should not be the only form of ongoing communication with them.

www.ingramcontent.com/pod-product-compliance
Lightning Source LLC
Chambersburg PA
CBHW061504180526
45171CB00001B/35